The Aeneid for Boys and Girls

By

Alfred J. Church

Contents

THE HORSE OF WOOD

The Greeks besieged the city of Troy for nearly ten years. They could not take it because the walls were so high and strong—some said that they had been built by the hands of gods—but they kept the Trojans inside. This had not always been so. There had been a time when the Trojans had gone out and fought with their enemies on the plain, sometimes they had beaten them in battle, and once they had very nearly burnt their ships. But this was all changed. They had lost some of the bravest of their chiefs, such as Hector, the best of the sons of Priam, and Paris the great archer, and many great princes, who had come from the countries round about to help them.

We can easily believe then that Priam, King of Troy, and his people were very glad to hear that one day the Greeks had gone home. Two Trojans, who had left the city two weeks or so before on a message from King Priam to one of his allies, came back saying that they had gone to the camp of the Greeks and had found it empty, and that there were no ships to be seen. Every one who was not ill or too old to move about made all the haste they could to get out of the city. The gates were opened wide for the first time during ten years, and men, women, and children hurried out to see the plain where so many battles had been fought, and the camp in which the enemy had lived, and the place where the ships had been dragged up on the shore. As you may suppose, those who had fought in the battles had a great deal to say about what they had done and what they had seen. There were many things to see, but the strangest one of all was a great Horse of Wood, which was standing not far from the walls of the city. No one was quite sure what it was, or what it meant. One man said: "It is a very curious thing. Let us drag it into the city that it may be a monument of all that we have suffered for the last ten years." Others said: "Not so; we had better burn it, or drag it down to the sea that the water may cover it, or cut it open to see whether there is anything inside." Of these no one was more vehement than Laocoön, priest of Neptune. "Take heed what you do, men of Troy," he cried. "Who knows whether the Greeks have really gone away? It may be that there are armed men inside this Horse; it may be that it has been made so big to overtop the walls of the city. Anyhow I am afraid of these Greeks, even when they give us gifts." And as he spoke, he threw the spear which he had in his hand at the Horse of Wood, and struck it on the side. A great rattling sound was heard, and the Trojans, if they had not been very blind and foolish, might have known that there was something wrong.

While the dispute was going on, some shepherds came up, bringing with them a man whose hands were bound behind his back. He had come out from a hiding-place, they said, of his own accord, when they were in the field. The young Trojans crowded round him, and began to mock at him, but he cried out in a very piteous voice: "What shall I do? where shall I go? the Greeks will not let me live, and the Trojans cry out for vengeance upon me." Then they began to pity him, and they bade him say who he was and what he had to tell.

Then the man turned to King Priam, and said: "I will speak the truth, whatever may happen to me. My name is Sinon, and I will not deny that I am a Greek. Perhaps you have heard of one Palamedes. The Greeks put him to death, saying that he was a traitor; but his only fault was that he wanted to have peace. Yes, they put him to death, and now that he is dead, they are sorry. I was a cousin of his, and my father sent me with him to Troy. So long as he prospered, I prospered also; but when he was done to death by the false witness of Ulysses, I fell into great grief and trouble, nor could I be silent; I swore that if ever I got back to Argos, I would have revenge on those who had brought him to his death. So Ulysses was always on the look-out to do me some harm; and at the last by the help of Calchas the prophet—but why do I tell you of these things? Doubtless you hold one Greek as bad as another. Kill me, if you will; only remember that this is the very thing which the two sons of Atreus wish, the very thing which Ulysses himself would give much money to secure."

Then the Trojans said: "Tell us more." And he went on. "Many times would the Greeks have gone home, for they were very tired of the war, but the sea was so stormy that they dared not go. Then they made this great Horse of Wood which you see, but the storms grew worse and worse. Then they sent to ask Apollo what they should do. And Apollo said: 'Men of Greece, when you came here you had to appease the winds with blood, and you must appease them with blood again when you go away.' Every one trembled when they heard this, for every one feared that it might be his blood that would be wanted. After a while Ulysses brought the prophet into the assembly of the people, and said: 'Tell us now who is it that the gods will have for a victim?' Then many thought that it was I against whom Ulysses was plotting. For nine days the prophet said nothing: 'He would not give any Greek,' he said, 'to death.' These were his words, but in truth he and Ulysses had plotted the whole thing between them. On the tenth day he spoke, and said: 'Sinon is the man.' To this all agreed, every man thinking, 'Well, it is not I that shall die.' So they fixed a day on which I was to be sacrificed, and made everything ready. But before it came, I broke my chains and escaped, hiding myself in the reeds of a pond, till they should set sail. And now I shall never see my own country again; no, nor my wife and children, and, doubtless, these cruel men will take vengeance on them because I escaped. And now I beseech you, O King, to have pity on me, for I have suffered much, though, indeed, I have not done harm to any man."

Then King Priam had pity on him and bade them unbind his hands, saying: "Forget your own people; from to-day you are one of us. But tell us now, why did the Greeks make this great Horse of Wood that we see?"

Then Sinon lifted up his hands to the sky and said: "O sun and moon and stars, I call you to witness that I have a good right to tell the secrets of my countrymen. Listen, O King. From the beginning, when the Greeks first came to this place, their hope has been in the help of Minerva. But she was angry with them for this cause. Ulysses and Diomed made their way into your city, and climbed into the citadel, and killed the guards. And then with hands all bloody from the slaughter, they laid hold of her image and carried it away. It was this that made the goddess angry, that they should dare to touch her with hands stained with blood. I saw with my own eyes how the eyes of the image, when these two brought it into the camp, flashed with anger, and how the drops of sweat stood upon it; yes, and how it leapt three times from the ground, shaking shield and spear. Then the prophet said: 'You must go back to Greece, and come again, and begin the war again, if you wish to take the city of Troy'—and this they are doing now; they have gone back to Greece, and they will soon return. Furthermore, he said: 'You must make a Horse of Wood to be a peace-offering to Minerva. Make it, I advise you, very great, so that the Trojans may not take it within their walls. For, if they do so take it, then you will never conquer their city. Nay, they will come to our own land, and lay siege to our cities, and our children will suffer the things which we have sought to bring on them. But if they hurt the thing, then they themselves shall perish.' "

This was the tale that Sinon told, and the Trojans believed it. Nor is this to be wondered at, because the gods themselves took part in deceiving them. For while Laocoön, the priest of Neptune, the same that had thrown his spear at the Horse, was sacrificing a bull on the altar of his god, two great serpents came across the sea from a certain island that was near. All the Trojans saw them come, with their heads raised high above the water, as is the way of snakes to swim. And when they reached the land they came on straight to the city. Their eyes were red as blood, and blazed like fire, and they made a dreadful hissing with their tongues. The Trojans grew pale with fear, and fled. But the serpents did not turn this way or that, but came straight to the altar at which Laocoön stood, with his two sons by him. And one serpent laid hold on one of the boys, and the other on the other, and they began to devour them. Then the father picked up a sword, and tried to help them, but they caught hold of him, and wound their folds round him. Twice did they wind themselves round his body and his neck, and their heads stood high above his head. And he still tried as hard as he could to tear them away with his hands, and the garlands which he bore, being a priest, dripped with blood. And all the time he cried aloud as a bull roars when the servant of the temple strikes him unskilfully, and he flies from the altar. And when the serpents had done their work, and both the priest and his sons were dead, then they glided to the hill on which stood the Temple of Minerva, and hid themselves under the feet of the image. And when the Trojans saw this, they said to themselves: "Now Laocoön has suffered the due reward of his deeds, for he threw his spear at the holy thing which belongs to the goddess, and now he is dead and his sons with him."

Then they all cried out together that the Horse of Wood should be drawn into the citadel. So they opened the great gate of the city, pulling down part of the wall that there might be more room, and they put rollers under the feet of the Horse, and they fastened ropes to it. Then they drew it into the city, boys and girls laying hold of the ropes, and singing songs with great joy. And every one thought it a great thing if he could put his hand to a rope. But there were not wanting signs of evil to come. Four times did the Horse halt as they dragged it, before it passed through the gate, and each time there might have been heard a great clashing of arms within. Also Cassandra opened her mouth, and prophesied the fate of the city; but no one took any heed of her words, for it was her doom that she should speak the truth and not be believed. So the Trojans drew the Horse of Wood into the city. That night they kept a feast to the gods with great joy, not knowing that the end of their city was now close at hand.

THE SACK OF TROY

Now the Greeks had only made a show of going away. They had taken their ships, indeed, from the place where they had been drawn up on the coast of Troy, but they had not taken them farther than a little island which was close by. There they hid themselves, ready to come back when the signal was given. When it was quite dark the signal was given; a burning torch was raised from the ship of King Agamemnon, which was in the middle of the fleet. When the Greeks saw this they got on board their ships, and rowed across from the island. The moon gave them light, and there was a great calm on the sea. At the same time Sinon opened the door in the Horse of Wood, and let out the chiefs who were hidden in it. And all the time the Trojans were fast asleep, not thinking of any danger.

Now Æneas, who was the chief hope and stay of the Trojans, had a dream. He dreamt that he saw Hector, the brave chief who had been killed by Achilles. He saw him not as he was in the old time, when he came back from the battle, bringing back the arms of Achilles, which he had taken from Patroclus; not as he was when he was setting fire to the ships, and the Greeks could not stand against him, but as he was when he lay dead. He was covered with dust and blood, and his feet were pierced through with thongs, for Achilles had dragged him at the wheels of his chariot three times round the walls of Troy.

When Æneas saw him he forgot all that had happened, and said: "Why have you been so long in coming? We have missed you much, and suffered much because you were not here to help us. But why do you look so miserable? Who has given you these wounds?"

To these questions the spirit made no answer. All that he said was this: "Fly, Æneas, fly, and save yourself from these flames. The enemy is inside our walls, and Troy is lost. The gods would have it so. If any one could have saved the city, I should have done it. But it was not to be.

You are now Troy's only hope. Take, then, the gods of your country, and flee across the sea; there some day you shall build another Troy."

And Æneas woke from his sleep, and while he lay thinking about the dream he heard a great sound, and it seemed to him like to the sound of arms. So he rose from his bed, and climbed on the roof, and looked at the city. Just so a shepherd stands upon a hill and sees, it may be, a great fire blown by a strong wind from the south, and sweeping over the corn-fields, or a flood rushing down from the mountains. As he looked he saw the fire burst out first from one great palace and then from another, till the very sea shone with the light of the burning city. Then he knew that what Hector had told him in the dream was true, that the Greeks had made their way into the city. So he put on his armour, though he did not know what he could do. Still, he thought to himself: "I may be able to help Troy in some way; anyhow, I can avenge myself on the enemy; at the least I can die with honour." Just as he was going out of his house the priest of Apollo met him. He was leading his little grandson by the hand, and on his other arm he was carrying an image of the god. When he saw Æneas he cried out: "O Æneas, the glory is gone from Troy; the Greeks have the mastery in the city. Armed men have come out of the Horse of Wood, and thousands have got in by the gates, which that traitor Sinon has opened." While he was speaking, others came up, one of them being young Corœbus, who had come to Troy, hoping to get the prophetess Cassandra for his wife. Æneas said to them: "Brothers, if you are willing to follow me to the death, come on. You see what has happened. The gods who used to guard our city have gone from it; nowhere is any help to be found. Still, we may die as brave men die in battle. Ay, and it may be that he who is willing to lose his life may save it." Then they all followed him, and they went through the city as fierce as hungry wolves when they come down from the mountains.

The first thing that happened was this. A certain Greek chieftain, who had many men with him, met them, and mistook them for his own countrymen. "Make haste, my friends!" he cried; "why are you so late? We are spoiling the city, and you have only just come from the ships." But when they made no answer, he looked again, and saw that he had fallen among enemies. So a man comes upon the snake among the rocks, and when it rises, with great swelling neck, he tries to fly. So the chieftain turned to fly, but the place was strange to him, and he and many of his company were killed. Then Corœbus said: "We have good luck, my friends. Let us now change our shields and put on the armour of the Greeks. Who can blame us for deceiving these Greeks?" Then he took the shield and helmet of the Greek chieftain, who had been slain, and his sword also. The others did the same, and so disguising himself he killed many of the Greeks. Others fled to the ships, and some climbed up again into the Horse of Wood.

As they went through the city they met a number of men who were dragging the prophetess Cassandra from the temple of Minerva, in which she had taken refuge. When Corœbus, who, as has been said, hoped to marry Cassandra, saw this, and how she lifted up her eyes to heaven—her hands she could not lift because they were bound with iron—he was mad with rage, and rushed at the men, seeking to set the girl free, and all the other Trojans followed him. Then there happened a very dreadful thing. There were many Trojans standing on the roofs of temples and houses close by; these men, when they saw Corœbus and the others with the Greek armour on them, which they had taken, took them for Greeks, and threw spears at them and killed many. And the Greeks also began to fight more fiercely than before, and those who had fled to the ships came back again. Altogether they gathered a great company together, and the Trojans, of whom there were but very few, could not stand up against them. Corœbus was killed first of all, and then almost all the others, good and bad, for it was the day of doom for the Trojans. At last Æneas was left with only two companions, one of them an old man, and the other hardly able to move for a wound which Ulysses had given him.

As he stood thinking what he should do, he heard a great shouting, and it seemed to come from the palace of King Priam. So he said to his companions: "Let us go and see whether we can help." And when they got there they found a fiercer battle than any that they had seen before in the city. Some of the Greeks were trying to climb up the walls. They had put ladders against them, and they stood on the steps high up, grasping the edge of the roof in one hand, and holding their shields with the other. And the Trojans, knowing that there was no hope of escaping, tore down the battlements and threw the big stones at the heads of the Greeks. Now Æneas knew of a secret way into the palace.

By this Hector's wife Andromaché had been used to come from Hector's palace, bringing her little boy with her to see his grandfather King Priam. So he was able to climb up on to the roof, without being seen by the Greeks, and to join his countrymen who were defending the palace. There was a high tower on the roof, so high that all the city of Troy could be seen from it, and the camp of the Greeks, and the ships. The Trojans broke away the foundations of this tower with bars of iron, and toppled it over, so that it fell upon the Greeks, and killed many of them. But the others pressed on just as fiercely as before, throwing javelins and stones and anything that came to their hands at the Trojans on the roof.

While some were trying to climb up on to the roof, others were breaking down the gates of the palace. The leader of them was the son of Achilles, Pyrrhus by name. He wore shining armour of bronze, and was as bright as a great snake which has slept in his hole all the winter, and when the spring begins, comes out with a new shining skin into the sunshine and lifts his head high and hisses with his forked tongue. He had a great battle-axe, which he held in both his hands, and with this he hewed through the doors; the very door-posts he broke down with it, making what one might call a great window, through which could be seen the great palace within, the hall of King Priam and of the kings who had reigned in Troy before him. And those who were inside also could see the armed men who were breaking in, and they made a great cry; and the women wailed and clung to the doors and pillars, and kissed them, because they thought that they should never see them any more. There were men who had been put to guard the gates, but they could not stop the son of Achilles, for he was as fierce and as strong as his father had been. He and his people were like to a river that is swollen with much rain and bursts its banks, and overflows all the plain. Just so did the Greeks rush into the palace.

When old King Priam saw the enemy in his hall he put on his armour. He had not worn it for many years, so old he was, but now he felt that he must fight for his home. And he took a spear in his hand, and would have gone against the Greeks. But his wife, Queen Hecuba, called to him from the place where she sat. She and her daughter and the wives of her sons had fled to the great altar of the gods of the household, and were clinging to it. They were like to a flock of doves which have been driven by a storm into a wood. The altar stood in an open court which was in the middle of the palace, and a great bay tree stood by, and covered it with its branches. When she saw how her husband had put on his armour, as if he were a young man, she cried to him, saying: "What has bewitched you that you have put on your armour? It is not the sword that can help us to-day; no, not if my own dear Hector, who was the bravest of the brave, were here. It is in the gods and their altars that we must trust. Come and sit with us; here you will be safe, or, at least, we shall all die together."

So she made the old man sit down in the midst of them. But lo! there came flying through the hall of the palace one of the sons of the king, Polites by name. Pyrrhus had wounded him, but the lad had fled, and Pyrrhus was close behind with his spear. And just as he came within sight of his father and his mother he fell dead upon the ground. When King Priam saw this he could not contain himself, but cried aloud, saying: "Now may the gods punish you for this wickedness, you who have killed a son before the eyes of his father and his mother. You say that you are a son of the great Achilles, but when you say it you lie. It was not thus that Achilles treated me. For when he had slain my son Hector, and I went to him to beg the body for burial, he gave it to me for due ransom, and sent me back to my own city without harm."

So did King Priam speak; then he took up a spear and cast it at Pyrrhus, but there was no strength in his blow. It did but shake the shield, not piercing it at all, and falling idly on the ground. Then said the son of Achilles: "Go, tell my father of his unworthy son, and of the wicked deeds which he doeth. And that you may tell him, die!" And as he spoke he caught the old man's white hair with his left hand and dragged him, slipping as he went in the blood of his son, to the altar, and with his right hand he lifted up his sword and drove it, up to the very hilt, into the old man's body. So died King Priam. Once he had ruled over many cities and peoples in the land of Asia, and now, after he had seen his city taken and his palace spoiled, he was slain and his carcass was cast out upon the earth, headless and without a name.

ÆNEAS AND ANCHISES

Aeneas from his place on the roof saw all these things, for they were done in the open court that was in the middle of the palace. He saw them, indeed, but he could give no help, being but one against many. But the sight of the old man lying dead made him think of his own father, and so of his wife Creüsa, and of his little son Ascanius, and how he had left them at home alone and without defence. As he thought to himself: "Shall I not return to them, for here I can do nothing?" he turned his eyes and saw Helen in the temple of Vesta. She was sitting by the altar, hoping to be safe in the holy place. She was greatly afraid, fearing the Trojans, upon whom she had brought ruin, and her husband whom she had deceived. When Æneas saw her he was full of rage; and he said to himself: "Shall this wicked woman go safe to Sparta? Shall she see again her home and her children, taking, it may be, women of Troy to be her handmaidens? Shall Troy be burnt and King Priam be slain, and she, who is the cause of all this trouble, come to no harm? It shall not be; I myself will kill her. There is no glory in such a deed; who can get honour from the death of a woman? Nevertheless I shall be taking vengeance for my kinsfolk and my countrymen."

But while he thought these things in his heart, there appeared to him his mother, Venus, in such a shape as he had never seen her before, not like to a woman of the earth, but tall and fair, as the gods who dwell in Heaven see her. Venus said to him: "What means this rage, my son? Have you no thought for me? Have you forgotten your old father Anchises, and your wife, and your little son? Surely the fire had burnt them up long ago, if I had not cared for them, and preserved them. And as for Helen, why are you angry with her? It is not she, it is not Paris, that has brought this great city of Troy to ruin; it is the anger of the gods. See now; I will take away the mist that is over your eyes. Look there; see how Neptune, god of the sea, is overthrowing the walls with his three-forked spear, and is rooting up the city from its foundations!

See there, again, how Juno stands in the great gate of the city, with a spear in her hand, and great hosts of Greeks from the ships! See how Minerva sits upon the citadel, with a storm cloud round her, and her awful shield upon her arm! See how Father Jupiter himself stirs up the enemies of Troy! Fly, my son; I will be with you, and will not leave you till you reach your father's house." When she had so spoken she vanished into the night.

Then Æneas looked, as his mother bade him, and saw the dreadful forms of gods, and how they were destroying the city, and all the place seemed, as he looked, to be sinking down into the fire. Just as an oak in the mountains, at which the woodmen cut with their axes, bows its head, with its branches shaking round about it, till at last, after bearing many blows, it falls at once, and crashes down the side of the mountain, so Troy seemed to fall. When he had seen this, he turned to go to his own home. His mother was by his side, though he could not see her, and he passed through the flames, and was not hurt, nor did the spear of the enemy wound him.

When he got to his home, he thought first of the old man, his father, and said to him: "Come now, let me carry you away from this city, to a safe place among the hills." But Anchises would not go. He did not wish to live in some strange country when Troy had been destroyed. "No," he said; "do you, who are strong and who have many days to live, fly. I will stay. If the gods had wished me to live, they would have preserved this place for me. It is enough for me, yea, more than enough, that already I have seen this city taken, and lived. Say good-bye to me, therefore, as you would say good-bye to a dying man. Death I will find myself, or, at least, the enemy will find it for me, when they come. Already I have lived too long."

So Anchises spoke, nor could they persuade him to change his mind, though his son, and his son's wife, and even the little child Ascanius begged him with many tears. When Æneas saw that he could not change the old man's purpose, he said to himself: "What shall I do? I will go back to the battle and die. Oh, my father, did you think that I would leave you and fly? This was a thing surely that you should never have said. If the gods will have it that nothing of Troy should be left; if it is your will that you and I and all your house should perish with the city; be it so. The way to bring this to pass is easy. Pyrrhus will soon be here, Pyrrhus red with the blood of King Priam, Pyrrhus who slays the son in the sight of his father, and the father at the altar. Was it for this, O Venus my mother, that you brought me safe through the flames, and thrust aside the spears of the enemy, that I might see my father and my wife and my son lie in one heap, slaughtered by the enemy? Comrade, give me my arms; we will go back to the battle, and die there, as brave men should."

Then he put on his armour, and took up his spear. But as he was going out of the door, his wife Creüsa threw herself on the ground and caught his feet. She held out to him the child Ascanius, and cried: "If you are going back to the battle that you may die there, then take your wife and child with you. For why should we live when you are dead? But if you have any hope that arms may help us, stay here, and guard your father and your wife and your son."

While she was speaking there happened a most wonderful thing. A fire was seen to shine upon the head of the child Ascanius, to play round his long curls, and to sparkle on his forehead. His father and his mother saw it, and were astonished. At first they thought that it was a real fire, and would have fetched water with which to put it out. But when the old man Anchises, who was wise in such matters, saw it, he was very glad, for he knew that this was no common fire, but a token of other things, that the child was dear to the gods. He looked up to heaven, and cried: "O Father Jupiter, if thou hearest prayer at all, hear me now, and give us a sign." While he was speaking, there was heard a great clap of thunder on the left hand, and a star was seen to shoot through the skies, leaving a long trail of light behind it, passing over the city, till it was hidden behind the woods of Ida. When the old man saw this he rose from the place where he was sitting, and bowed his head, and said: "I will make no more delay; lead on, and I will follow; O gods of my country, save my house, and my grandson. This sign came from you."

Then said Æneas, for the fire was coming nearer, and the light growing brighter, and the heat more fierce: "Climb, dear father, on my shoulders; I will carry you, nor shall I be tired by the weight. We will be saved, or we will perish together. The little Ascanius shall go with me, and my wife shall follow behind, but not too near." Then he turned to the servants, and said: "Men of my house, listen to me. You know that as one goes out of the city there is a tomb and a temple of Ceres in a lonely place, with an old cypress tree close by. That is the place where we will meet. Each by different ways, not all together, that we may not be seen by the enemy. And do you, my father, take in your hands the images of the household gods. My hands are red with blood, and I must not touch holy things till I have washed them in running water."

Then he put a lion's skin upon his shoulders and stooped down, and the old man Anchises climbed upon them. And the boy Ascanius laid hold of his hand, keeping pace with his father as best he could with his little steps. And Creüsa followed behind. So he went, with many fears. He had not been afraid of the swords and spears of the enemy, but now he was full of fear for them who were with him, father and wife and child. But when he had nearly got to the gates of the city there happened a dreadful thing. There was heard a great sound of feet in the darkness; and the old man cried: "Fly, my son, fly; they are coming. I see the flashing of shields and swords." So Æneas hurried on, but his wife was separated from him. Whether she lost her way, or whether she was tired and sat down to rest herself, no one knew. Only Æneas never saw her again; nor did he know that she was lost, till all the company met at the appointed place, and she alone was not among them. It seemed a most grievous thing to him, and he made loud complaints against both gods and men. Then he told his comrades that they must take care of the old man and of Ascanius, and that he would go and search for his wife. So he went first to the gate by which he had come out of the city. Then he went to his house, thinking that by some chance she might have gone back there. He found the house indeed, but the Greeks were there, and it was nearly burnt. After this he went to the citadel and to the palace of King Priam. Her he saw not, but he saw in the temple of Juno Ulysses and Phœnix keeping guard over the spoil, treasure from the temples, and cups of gold, and beautiful robes, and long lines of prisoners, women and children. And still he looked for his wife, going through all the streets of the city, and calling her name aloud. While he was doing this her image seemed to stand before him. It was she, and yet another, so tall and beautiful did she seem. And the spirit said: "Why are you troubled? These things have come about by the will of the gods. Jupiter himself has ordered that your Creüsa should not sail across the seas with you. You have a long journey to make, and many seas to cross till you come to the land of Hesperia, to the place where the river Tiber flows softly through a fair and fertile land. There you shall have great prosperity, and shall marry a wife of royal race. Weep not for your Creüsa, and do not think that I shall be carried away to be the bond slave of some Greek lady. Such a lot would not be fitting for one who comes, as I come, from the race of the kings of Troy and for her who was the daughter-in-law of Venus. The mother of the gods keeps me in this land to be her servant. And now farewell. Think sometimes of me, and love the child Ascanius, for he is your child and mine."

So spake the spirit; but when Æneas would have answered, it vanished out of his sight. Three times did he try to put his arms round her, and three times it seemed to slip away from him, being thin and light as air. And now the night was far spent and the morning was about to break. So he went back to his comrades and found, much to his joy, that there were many more than he had hoped to find, a great company of men and women, all ready to follow him wherever he might lead them. And now the morning star, which goes before the sun, rose over Mount Ida, and Æneas, seeing that the Greeks were in possession of Troy, and that there was no hope of help, again took his father on his shoulders, and went his way to the mountains, his people following him.

OF THE VOYAGE OF ÆNEAS

I

As long as the Greeks remained in the land of Troy, Æneas and his friends lay hid among the hills. But they had not to do this for very long. The Greeks were glad enough to go to their homes, which they had not seen for ten years. So they put the spoils which they had taken out of the city, with the prisoners, into their ships, and set sail. Then the Trojans came out of their hiding-places, and began to cut down pine trees on Mount Ida—this was the name of the biggest of the hills, among which they had taken refuge—and to build ships. They had made up their minds to leave the land of Troy, and to find a new home somewhere else. This was the second time that the city had been destroyed, and the place seemed to be unlucky. By this time a great number of people had come together. Some had escaped in one way or another from the city; some had been sold as slaves, and had run away from their masters, or had been set free. Many ships, therefore, had to be built; but in the spring all was ready, and they set sail; very sorry they were to go, for they were leaving their country for ever, and they did not know where they should find another home.

They had sailed but a very little way when they came to a country called Thrace. For a time they thought that this was just the place which they wanted. The Thracians had been very good friends to Troy in former times. While the war was going on many of their warriors had come to fight for King Priam. So Æneas began to make a plan for a city, laying the foundation, and marking out the lines of streets and squares. But while he was busy with these things, he found out in a very strange way, that a very dreadful deed had been done by the King of Thrace, and that he had better go away as fast as he could. What had happened was this. While Troy was still standing, King Priam had sent away one of his sons, and with him a very large quantity of gold, to the King of Thrace. This man was an old friend, and Priam thought to himself: "If anything should happen to Troy and to me, still there would be something safe. There would be the boy to keep up the old name, and he would have plenty of money to help him." But when Troy was taken by the Greeks this wicked king murdered the poor boy, and kept the gold for himself. When Æneas found this out, he said to himself, "A country where such wicked things are done is no home for us," and he set sail again.

The next place which he came to was an island called Delos. Once, it was said, it had been a floating island, but then it was fixed and firm, and it was the place where Apollo and his sister dwelt, who were the same, as men believed in those days, as the sun and the moon. Here there was a very famous temple of Apollo, and the priest of the temple was also the king of the island. Now Apollo had always been a friend to Troy, and when the priest knew who the strangers were that had come to the island, he went to meet them, and gave them a kind welcome, and took Æneas into his own palace. Then Æneas thought to himself: "I will ask the god to tell where I should go." So he went to the temple, and made an offering according to custom, and said: "O Apollo, hear me, for thou wert always a friend to Troy. Give, I pray thee, a place where we, who alone are left, may rest, a land of our own, and a kingdom that shall endure for ever. Tell us whither we should go, whom we should follow, and what we may look for. And speak plainly, I beseech thee, so that I may understand." Scarcely had he ended these words, when there was heard a loud rumbling sound, and the temples, and the laurel grove which stood about it, and the very hills around, were shaken. After this there came from out the middle of the temple a clear voice, speaking these words: "Sons of Troy, go boldly forth; seek the land where your fathers, who lived in the old time were born; the country which first sent you out shall welcome you again; then the house of Æneas shall grow and prosper till it shall reign over the whole world."

Great was the joy with which Æneas and his followers heard these words. But then they began to think to themselves: "What is the land of our fathers? what is its name? where is it?" nor could any one answer these questions till old Anchises, after much turning of the matter over in his mind, said: "My children, be not troubled or doubtful any more. I

23

know the meaning of what the god has told us. There is a famous island in the southern part of this sea where now we are, and its name is Crete. This is the place where great Jupiter himself was born, and it is sacred to him. Far and wide it reaches; there are a hundred cities in it; and there is a Mount Ida, even as there is in our own land of Troy. It is from this island of Crete that our fathers came in old time. One Teucer was their chief; he came to the land which we have just left, and dwelt in it in the old days before Troy was built. Let us set sail without delay, having first made such offerings as it is meet to make. If the winds be favourable, we shall come to Crete on the third morning from now." So they made the offerings; one bull to Neptune, god of the sea; another to Apollo; a white sheep to the gentle winds, and a black one to the stormy. They knew, too, that the King of Crete, who was one of those that had come to fight against Troy, had been banished; and they were glad to think that they should not find an enemy in the country.

When these things were done, Æneas and his men set out. They set their sails, and rowed with their oars, and the sailors shouted "Crete!" "Crete!" so glad were they to think that they were about to find a home. In due time they came to the island. And here again Æneas, being quite sure that he had found the right place, began to make plans for a city. In Thrace he had called it Ænos after himself; but this was to be Pergamos, for this had been the name of the citadel in old Troy. But after a time everything seemed to go wrong. The air seemed to be poisoned, and the winds that blew seemed to parch the grass and to blast the corn. The cattle were destroyed by plague, and some of the people died, while nearly all suffered from fever and agues. All this greatly grieved Æneas, and he made up his mind to go to Delos and ask Apollo whether he had made any mistake and whither he really ought to go.

That very night, when all were asleep, he only being awake, for he was in too great trouble to sleep, he saw before him in the light of the moon, which was shining through the window of his room, the household gods which he had carried away from Troy. Quite plainly did he see them, and he heard them say these words: "What you are going to Delos to ask, Apollo bids us tell you here. We are the gods whom you saved out of the ruins of burning Troy; we are your companions; we share your fate, we will bring you to the country which is meant for you, and from which your children's children will rule the world.

Do not grow weary of wandering. You must look for another home, for Crete is not the place in which Apollo told you to dwell. There is a country called Hesperia, the land of the West; it is an ancient land; its people are strong and brave. That is our proper home; it was from this that our first father came. Tell this then to the old man, your father, that Apollo bids you go to Hesperia which men also call Italy. As for Crete, it is not meant for you."

Æneas lay in his bed and listened in a great fear, for he saw the gods quite plainly and not at all as if he were dreaming. Then he got up from his bed, prayed and offered sacrifice, and afterwards went and told his father what he had seen and heard. The old man said: "I was wrong when I said that Crete was the place from which our fathers came. And now I remember that in the days when Troy still stood Cassandra used to speak about Hesperia and Italy. But who would have thought that we who dwelt in Asia should ever go to the land of the West? And no one at that time believed the things which Cassandra spoke. But now let us obey the commands of Apollo and depart."

So the Trojans put all that they had on board their ships and departed. As soon as they were out of sight of land a great storm arose. The wind blew fiercely, and the waters were like mountains, and there was much thunder and lightning. For three days they did not see the sun, and for three nights they did not see the stars, nor did they know where they were. On the fourth day they came in sight of land, with hills, and smoke rising as it might be from the houses of men. So the sailors rowed with all their might and soon brought the ships to land.

They found that it was a pleasant island, with fields in which there were herds of oxen and flocks of goats feeding; but they could not see any one who was looking after them. By this time the Trojans were very tired and hungry; so they took some of the oxen and of the goats, and killed them, and cooked their flesh. Also they fetched wine from their ships, and sat down, and began to eat and drink. But they did not know what the place to which they had come really was or what kind of creatures lived there. These creatures were called Harpies, a name which means "Snatchers." These were wicked women who had been changed into a horrible kind of birds. They were like vultures which feed on dead bodies, and they had the wings of birds, and claws instead of hands; they had the faces of women, but with a look on them as if they were starving. Suddenly, then, the Trojans, while eating and drinking, heard a great noise of wings, and in a moment the Harpies had come down, and snatched the flesh which the men were eating, and carried it off; and what they did not carry off they made so dirty that no one could bear to have it near him. Then the Trojans went to another place, which was close to a rock, and so sheltered in a way. There they made another dinner ready; but scarcely had they begun to eat, when the Harpies came down again—whether from the same place as before or from another no one knew—and snatched away the meat again, and spoilt what was left. Then the Trojans went to a third spot, and prepared their food; only this time they hid their swords and spears in the grass by their sides. When they saw the Harpies come again, they jumped up and laid hold of the swords and spears and tried to kill the creatures. But it was of no use; their skin was too hard to be wounded; the steel could not be driven through the feathers. Still, though they could not be killed, they were driven away, and flew to their holes among the cliffs. Only one remained; this settled on a rock out of the reach of the men, and said these words in a man's voice:

"Listen; was it not enough that you should kill our cattle? Will you drive us away from our own island? Hear my words, for these are the words of fate. This is what the gods, Jupiter and Apollo, whom you think to be your friends, decree. You will come at last to the land of Italy; that is settled. But know that before you build the walls of your new city you will be so hungry that you will be driven to eat the very tables on which you set your meat."

When the dreadful creature had said these words, she flew away. Then the old man Anchises lifted up his hands to the skies, and prayed that these things might not come upon them or might be turned to their good.

II

That very day Æneas and his people sailed away from the land of the Harpies. They passed by many islands of the Greeks, Ithaca among them, which was the country of Ulysses. "A bad place," they said, as they passed, "and the home of a bad man." Not far from here they spent the winter, and then, turning to the west, they came to a country that was called Epirus. And here Æneas heard from some one who lived in those parts a marvellous thing, namely, that there was not far away a city which had a Trojan king, and that this king was a son of Priam, and that his wife was Andromaché, whose first husband was the brave Hector. Then Æneas said to himself: "I will go and see whether this strange tale that they tell me is true." So he went his way to the city, and when he came near it, he saw a river, and asked someone that passed by, "What is the name of this river?" And the man said, "This is the Simoïs." Now there is a river Simoïs that runs through the plain of Troy. A little farther on he saw a grove, and in the grove an altar, and by the altar stood Andromaché. She was making offerings to the spirit of Hector, and wept much as she made them. When she saw Æneas, and knew his arms, for they were what the Trojans used to wear, she was very much afraid, and fainted. When she came to herself, she said: "Is this that I see real, or is it a dream? Is it Æneas whom I see? Are you alive? And, if you are dead, where is my Hector?" Æneas said: "Yes, lady, I am alive; this is flesh and blood that you see, not a ghost. And you? what has happened to you? are you still the wife of Pyrrhus?"

Andromaché answered: "Truly there was but one among the daughters and the daughters-in-law of Priam that was happy! she whom the Greeks slew at the tomb of Achilles. As for me, who once had Hector for my husband, I was carried across the sea as a slave is carried. A slave I was, though they called me a wife. And when Pyrrhus wished to marry the daughter of Helen, then he gave me to Helenus, as one slave is given to another. But Pyrrhus was slain by Orestes, who loved the daughter of Helen. And when he was dead, his kingdom was divided, and part of it came to Helenus, this country where we now are. He has built a town and called it Pergamos, and the river he has called Simoïs. But tell me, how came you here? was it by chance, or did a storm drive you out of your course? or did the gods send you? And your boy Ascanius, is he alive and well? Is he strong and brave? He should be such, if he has Æneas for his father, and Hector for his uncle."

While these two were talking Helenus came from the city and a great train of people with him, and bade Æneas and his company welcome. And he showed him all the place, and how everything had been made as like to Troy as might be. Only at Troy all things were large, and here all things were small. Afterwards Helenus made a great feast in his palace, and they ate and drank and were merry.

After a few days had passed, Æneas, seeing that the wind was favourable for his journey, said to Helenus: "It is time for us to go. Tell me now, for you are a wise man, and know what is going to happen, shall we prosper? It is the gods who bid us take this journey, and all things seem to promise well. But it has been prophesied to us that we shall have to bear dreadful hunger. Tell me then what I should do, and what I should avoid, and for what I should prepare."

Then said Helenus to Æneas: "Let us come to the temple of Apollo. There, I hope, the god will put into my mouth the answer to the questions which you ask."

So they went to the temple of Apollo. And when they had offered sacrifice and prayed, the spirit of the god came into the heart of Helenus, and he prophesied: "Son of Venus, be sure that it is according to the will of the gods that you are making this journey. Listen then to me, and learn what you must do that you may come safely to the land where you would be, even to Italy. Some things I do not know, and some that I know I may not speak, for Juno forbids, but what I may say is this: First know that you have yet a long way to go, and many seas to cross. It is true that Italy is not far from us even here; but it is not in these parts that you will find your home. Those evil men, the Greeks, are here, and you cannot find a dwelling-place among them. And this shall be a sign to you that you have come to the right place. You will find a white sow with thirty little pigs about her. As to the eating of your tables which the Harpy prophesied, be not troubled; Apollo will help you. Sail, therefore, southward from this place, and pass by the shore which you will see on your right hand, though it is the shore of Italy. And when you have passed it to the very end, you will come to the island of Sicily. There you will see a narrow strait which divides the two; in old time they were one, but now the sea flows between them. Venture not into this strait; it is a terrible place. On the right hand is Scylla in her cave, and on the left hand is the whirlpool of Charybdis. Scylla is a dreadful creature. In part of her she is like a fair woman, and in part she is like a monster of the sea, and she has six heads like to a wolf's head. Go, therefore, all round the island of Sicily. It is a long journey, but it is safe. And when you come to the other shore of Italy, that which lies to the setting of the sun, then sail northward. And remember at all times, and in all places, to do honour to Juno, that so you may win her favour. And you will come to a place called Cumæ; there dwells a wise woman whose name is the Sibyl. Apollo speaks by her mouth, even as he speaks by mine. Inquire of her, and she will tell you all that you should know, what wars you must wage, and what dangers you must endure, and what you may avoid. These things I may not speak, but you shall hear them from her. And now depart in peace; and wherever you go, remember that you are a son of Troy, and make the Trojan name to be great under heaven."

Then the prophet told his people to bring gifts for his departing friends, gold, and carvings of ivory, and caldrons, and a coat of chain mail, and a helmet with a plume, which Pyrrhus himself had worn. Horses also he gave, and tackling for the ships, and arms for the men. Also he gave Æneas guides who knew the way. And he bade them all a kind farewell, especially the old man Anchises, as one whom he should not see again. Andromaché also came, bringing a Phrygian cloak for Ascanius, and other fine things for him to wear. And she said to the boy: "Take these things to show that she who was once Hector's wife loves you well. Yes, for you are the very image of my own dear boy, whom they killed so cruelly. Your eyes and face and hands are like his, and indeed, if he were alive, he would be of the same age as you." Then Æneas bade them farewell: "Happy you," he said, "whose wanderings are finished, who have found your rest. You have no seas to cross; you have not to seek this land of Italy, which seems to fly before us, as we follow it. You have another Troy here before your eyes. Farewell, and know that if ever I come to this land of Italy, there shall be friendship between you and me, and between your children and my children forever."

After this they sailed away. And when it was night, they drew their ships to land, and slept upon the shore, but at midnight the chief pilot, whose name was Palinurus, roused himself and looked up at the sky, and took a note of the weather. And when he saw that the stars were bright, the Great Bear and the Little Bear, and Orion, with his belt of gold, he thought to himself: "These these are signs of fair weather; we will not lose the time." So he blew the trumpet which was a signal for starting. And all the men awoke and launched their ships. Through the darkness they rowed, and when the morning was growing red in the east, they looked, and behold! there was a land with hills to be seen far away, and a shore lying low. Then the old man Anchises cried, "This is the land of Italy." And he filled a great golden cup with wine, and standing on the stern poured it out, saying: "Gods of the sea and of the land, give us fair winds and an easy journey."

But when they came so near that they could see what was on the shore, the old man looked again, and saw four white horses, and he said: "What the prophet said was true. This is a land of enemies; for a horse is a sign of war; still, because horses may be trained to obey and to bear the bit, we will hope that after war there will be peace."

Then the Trojans trimmed their sails, and bore to the right, that is westward, lest some enemy should set upon them, for they knew that there were Greeks in the land. After a while they came to the place of which Helenus had told them. And when Anchises heard the roaring of the sea and saw how the waves seemed to rise up to the very sky, he said: "Here is Scylla, and here is Charybdis. Row, my comrades, row with all your might." This they did, and Palinurus, the pilot, being in the foremost ship, steered to the left, and all the other ships followed him. And the sailors rowed as hard as they could, and at last, as the sun was setting, they came to a quiet harbour, well sheltered from the sea. Into this they brought their ships, and would have rested during the night. But Mount Ætna was close by, and from it there came, without ceasing, thunders, and clouds of smoke, and showers of stones, and a great flood of melted rocks. The story is that a great giant lies under the mountain. He rebelled against Jupiter, and Jupiter laid him under the mountain as a punishment. And when he is tired of lying on one side, they say, he turns to the other, and the whole land is shaken. But the Trojans knew nothing of the matter, and they lay trembling all the night.

In the morning they saw some one coming to them out of the wood which was close by. He was a most miserable creature to look at; his clothes were nothing but rags, fastened together with thorns, and he seemed to be half dying of hunger. They knew, when they saw him, that he was a Greek, and he knew them to be Trojans. For a little time he stood, as if he would have run away; but then ran as fast as he could, and threw himself on his knees, crying out: "Men of Troy, I pray you by the stars and by the gods, and by the air which you breathe, take me away from this dreadful place. Take me whither you choose; or, if you will, drown me in the sea. I confess that I am a Greek; I confess that I fought against Troy. If I must die, let me at least die by the hands of men."

And he caught hold of Æneas by the knees. And Æneas said: "Who are you? how come you to be in this plight?"

Thy man answered: "I am a man of Ithaca, and I went to the war against Troy with Ulysses. And as we were going home, we came to this land. And Ulysses wished to see who dwelt here. So he took twelve of his men, of whom I was one. We came to a great cave, and found that it was the home of a shepherd. And Ulysses said: 'It is a rich shepherd that lives here; let us stay till he comes; maybe he will give us something.' But when he came, lo! he was a dreadful, man-eating giant. He shut us up in the cave, and devoured two of us that night, and two the next morning, and two again for his supper. But after his supper Ulysses gave him wine to drink, and made him tipsy; and put out his eye—he had one only in the middle of his forehead—as he lay asleep. The next day the others escaped, but I was left. And now I say, fly as soon as you can from this place; for this monster, indeed, may not harm you, for he is blind, but there are a hundred others, as big as he and as cruel, who live in this land. Flee, therefore, I say, and either kill me or take me with you." While he was speaking the Cyclops, that is to say, Round Eye, came in sight, with his flocks following him. He was a horrible creature to behold, very big and shapeless and blind. He came down to the sea, and waded out, and though he went many yards from the shore, yet the waves did not come up to his middle, and he washed the place where his eye had been, grinding his teeth the while. Then the Trojans, taking the Greek on board, pushed off from the land, and the monster heard the sound of their rowing, and shouted aloud to his fellows. They hurried down to the shore, and the Trojans saw them stand, tall as a grove of oaks or cypresses. Then, by favour of the gods, a north wind blew and carried them away, and they sailed on till they came to the southernmost part of the island, and after that to a place which men call Drepănum, that is to say, the reaping hook, for the harbour is of the shape of such a hook. There the old man Anchises died and was buried.

THE SHIPWRECK

Not many days after the burial of Anchises Æneas and his companions set sail. Now the goddess Juno hated the Trojans for many reasons, the chief of which was this. There was a certain city which she greatly loved, Carthage by name. It was just then being built by Queen Dido, and Juno hoped, if it might be possible, to make it the first city in the world. But she had been told that this could not be done, that the first city in the world would be one that the Trojans would build in Italy. And now she saw these very Trojans sailing from Sicily to this same land of Italy. They had wandered, as we have seen, for several years, and now they were about to find a home. She was very angry to see this, and said to herself: "Am I then to be disappointed? Shall I not be able to keep these Trojans from settling in Italy? Minerva burnt a whole fleet of Greeks, and drowned the men, because she was angry with one of them, even Ajax. She took Jupiter's own thunderbolts, and broke the ships with them. As for Ajax, she caught him up in a whirlwind, and dashed him upon the sharp point of a rock, so that he was pierced through. She could do this, and I, though I am Jupiter's own wife and sister, can do nothing against these Trojans! Who will honour me? Who will offer sacrifices to me, if I can do nothing?"

Then she went to a certain rocky island where Æolus, the king of the winds, lived. He had a great prison there in which he kept the winds under bolt and bar. This he had been set to do by Jupiter because if they were not so kept in they would blow away heaven and earth in their rage. Juno said to him: "King Æolus, Jupiter has given you the kingdom of the winds that you may do with them as you will. A nation which I hate is sailing across the sea from Sicily to Italy. Loose the winds upon them, and drown their ships in the sea. And now hear what I will give you if you will do this. I have twelve beautiful nymphs that wait on me; the most beautiful of them you shall have for your wife."

King Æolus said: "O mighty Juno, it is for you to speak and for me to obey. It is of your kindness that I am king of the winds, and that I am allowed to sit at the table of the gods." As he spoke he struck the great gates of the prison with his spear, and broke them in. In a moment the winds rushed out, and swept across the sea, making great waves before them. It was not long before they reached the Trojans' ships, for the island of Æolus was near to where they were sailing. In a moment the sky was hidden, and the day became as dark as the night, and there were lightnings and thunders all about.

When Æneas saw all this he grew cold with fear. He was not afraid of spears and swords in the battle, but it was a wretched thing, he thought, to be drowned. "O happy they," he cried, stretching out his hands, "who fell under the walls of Troy, before their fathers' eyes! O Diomed, bravest of the great, I would that you had slain me, even as Hector was slain by the spear of Achilles, and many a brave Trojan with him, whose bodies the river Simoïs rolled down to the sea!"

While he was speaking, a great gust of wind struck the sails of his ship from behind, and turned it broadside to the waves. Three other ships were tossed on to certain rocks which are in those parts. Men call them altars because they are flat, and sometimes they are covered with the waves, and sometimes they show above them. Three ships were tossed upon quicksands which were in those parts, and others were sadly shattered by the waves. And one was sunk outright. This was the one in which the Lycians with their chief Orontes sailed. The Lycians were friends of the Trojans, and had come a long way to help them, and were now going with them in their wanderings. Æneas was very sorry to see the broken planks, and the precious things floating about, and a few men swimming in the waves, for most of them were drowned.

It was not long before Neptune, the ruler of the sea, heard the noise of the winds and waves, where he sat in his palace at the bottom of the sea. He lifted his head above the waves, and saw how the ships were scattered, and he knew that his sister Juno had done this because she hated the Trojans. He called with a loud voice, which could be heard even above the storm, and said: "What is this that you are do-ing, O winds? Why are you troubling Heaven without my leave? I will—but I had best make the sea calm again; only be sure that if you do this again you will be punished. Go and tell your king that it is I who am the king of the sea, not he; let him keep to his rocks and make the winds obey him."

Then he commanded the waves to be still; also he scattered the clouds, and he brought back the sun. At his bidding other gods of the sea came to help. They lifted the ships off the rocks, and drew them out of the quicksands. And when this had been done he commanded that his chariot should be brought, and he rode in it across the sea, and as he went a great calm fell upon it. It was just as happens when there is a riot in a city, and the people are furious, and throw stones and burning torches about, till suddenly there comes among them some one whom they all honour; a good man and true. When he speaks they all listen to him, and the riot ceases.

Then Æneas and his companions made for the nearest shore. And this was the land of Africa, for they had been driven far out of their course. There they found a harbour running far into the land, so far that the water is quite calm within; on either side were high cliffs, and woods upon them. At the far end of the harbour was a cave, and a spring of sweet water. To this place Æneas came, with seven ships, all the rest being scattered about. Right glad were they to stand again on dry land. And one of them struck a spark out of a flint, and they lighted a fire with leaves and dry branches. They took also some of the wheat which they had with them in the ships, and parched it by the fire, and ground it, making it fit to eat. While they were doing this, Æneas climbed a hill which was close by, thinking that he might see some of the other ships. These he could not see, but he saw below him three great stags, and a herd of deer following them. Then he took the bow and the arrows which his companion, Achates by name, was carrying, and let fly. He killed the three great stags, and four out of the herd, making seven, one for each ship. These the men fetched. Also they took wine out of the ships; for King Acestes, who had entertained them in Sicily, had given them a good store of wine to take with them. So they made ready to feast. Some of the deer's flesh they broiled on spits, and some they boiled in water. And they drank of the wine, and were not a little comforted. And after supper they talked of their friends who were absent, wondering whether they were alive or dead.

CARTHAGE

The next day Æneas set forth to see what the land to which they had come might be. First he hid the ships in a bay which was well covered with trees, and then he went, and Achates with him. In each hand he carried a spear with a broad point. As he went his mother Venus met him. She had taken the shape of a girl, wearing the dress of a Spartan huntress. On her shoulders she carried a bow, and her hair was loose, and her tunic was short to the knees, and her upper garment fastened with a knot. The false huntress said to them:

"Stranger, tell me whether you have seen one of my sisters hereabouts. She has a bow and a quiver, and has the skin of a spotted lynx round her."

Æneas answered: "O lady, I have not seen such an one as you speak of! Lady, I call you, but you seem to be more than mortal woman, such is your look and such your voice. Surely you must be a goddess, perhaps the sister of Phœbus, or one of the nymphs who wait upon her. Whoever you are, look kindly on us, and help us. Tell us now what is this land to which the winds have driven us, for we know not what it is, or who dwell in it."

Venus said: "I am no goddess as you think, stranger. It is the custom for us girls of Tyre to carry a bow and a quiver, and to wear the dress of a huntress. For it is a Tyrian city to which I belong though the country is Africa. Our queen is Dido, and she came to this land from Tyre, flying from the wicked king, who was brother to her husband. This husband was a certain Sichæus, who was the richest of the Tyrians, and there was great love between him and his wife. But the king of the country was very greedy after gold, and he made a quarrel with his brother Sichæus, and took him unaware, even when he was doing sacrifice at the altar, and killed him. For a long time the king hid the matter from Dido, saying that he had sent her husband on some great business from which he would get much honour, and that he would soon come again. But at last she saw in her dreams the likeness of her husband, and he showed her his wounds, and told her how he had been killed. Then he bade her fly from the land as quickly as she could, and he told her of a place where much treasure, silver and gold and precious stones, was hidden in the earth. So Dido made everything ready for flight, and when she looked for companions, she found many; for not a few hated the king, and not a few feared him. So they laid hold of certain ships that were ready—and there were many ships at Tyre—and laded them with gold, and fled across the sea. And all this was done by the leading of a woman, even Dido. So they came to this place, where they are building the city of Carthage. So much land did Queen Dido buy from the king of the country as could be enclosed with a bull's hide. Only know that they cut the bull's hide into many strips, so that they could enclose a large space with it. And now tell me; whence do you come, and whither are you going?"

Æneas answered: "O lady, if I should tell all my story, the night would fall before I could come to an end. We are men of Troy; we have wandered over many seas for now seven years, and have been driven by a storm on to this land of Africa. As for me, men call me Æneas. My race is of Jupiter himself, and the land which I seek is Italy. With twenty ships did I set sail from the island of Sicily, going on the way on which the gods sent me. Twenty ships I had, and now I have but seven; Europe and Asia have cast me out, and now I am wandering over the desert plains of Africa." Venus answered him: "Do not think, stranger, whoever you are, that the gods are against you; they are your friends if they have brought you to this city of Carthage. Go on, therefore, and show yourself to Queen Dido. As for your ships and your companions, do not be afraid, for they are safe. Look up now into the sky. Do you not see those twenty swans, flying happily in the air? See now an eagle swoops down upon them, and they are scattered. You look again; they are in order once more, and now they are coming down to the earth, and some are settling on the ground, and some are about to settle. So shall it be with your ships."

When the false huntress had said this, she turned away, and there seemed to shine a rosy light from her neck as she turned, and there was a sweet smell, as of some heavenly perfume, and the tunic that was short to the knee seemed to grow to her feet. Then Æneas perceived that she was indeed his mother, and he cried: "O my mother, why do you mock me again and again with these false shows? Why do you not let me put my hand in yours and speak with you face to face?" Then he went on towards the city, and Achates with him. But no one could see them, for Venus covered them with a mist lest any should stop them to inquire their business or hinder them in any way. So the two hastened on, and they came to a hill which overlooked the city, and they saw how great and fine it was, with high gates and broad streets, and a great multitude of men and women walking to and fro. Some were building the walls and the citadel, and others marked out the places where houses should be built. Also they were choosing judges and magistrates. And some digged harbours, for Carthage was to be, as Tyre, a city of many ships, and others laid the foundations of a theatre, and cut out columns from the rock to make it fine to look at. They were like bees in the early summer. The young swarms go out from the hive, and they labour, filling the cells with honey, and some take the loads from those that come back, and others keep off the drones. When Æneas saw them, he cried: "Happy men who have found a city to dwell in!"

Now there was in the very middle of the city a thick wood of trees. Here, when Dido and her people had first come to the place, there had been digged out of the ground a horse's head; and when they saw it, they were very glad, for it had been told them that this should be a sign to them of good things, namely that their city should be great in war, and should have great riches. Here Dido was building a great temple to Juno. Very splendid it was, with door-posts and gates of bronze, and a great flight of steps leading to it. Into this temple Æneas and Achates entered, and he saw upon the walls pictures of the battles which the Trojans and Greeks had fought at Troy. Then Æneas said to his companion: "Is there any land which is not filled with our troubles? Yet it is good to know that these are not barbarians, that they have praise to give to courage, and tears for the sorrows of men. Fear not, my friend. It will be good for us that these people know what we have done and suffered." Then he turned to look at the paintings which were upon the walls, and was well pleased to see them. In one he saw how the Trojans were driving the Greeks before them, and in another how they were flying from Achilles. Also he saw the white tents of Rhesus, King of

Thrace, who came to help the Trojans, and was slain by Diomed, and his horses driven to the camp of the Greeks, before they had eaten the grass of the Trojan plains or drunk of their streams. For it had been prophesied that if they should do this but once, Troy never should be taken. Also they saw how Troilus had met Achilles in battle, and had been conquered by him, for, indeed, he was no match for him. There he lay dead in his chariot, his hand holding still the reins, but his head and shoulders were dragged upon the earth, and the point of his spear made a trail in the dust. In another place the Trojan women went as suppliants to the temple of Minerva, taking a most beautiful robe for an offering; they stood before the goddess, beating their breasts, but the goddess turned away her head. Also he saw Achilles dragging the body of Hector round the walls of Troy. In another place he was selling the body for gold. Æneas groaned to see the man whom he had loved, and old Priam the king, whom he had himself beheld slain by Pyrrhus. And he saw, moreover, himself fighting in the midst of the Greek chiefs; also black Memnon, son of the morning, who had come from the eastern land to help the Trojans, bringing a great host with him, and the Queen of the Amazons, and her warrior women with her, all of them carrying shields shaped like the moon. She was very fierce to look at; one of her breasts was bare, and she had a girdle of gold about her. She was but a girl, yet she dared to fight with men.

DIDO

While Æneas was looking at these pictures, Queen Dido herself came, with a great crowd of youths following her. She was the most beautiful of women. Not Diana herself could be more fair to look at when she dances with the nymphs, by head and shoulders taller than them all. When Dido came to the gate of the temple, she sat down upon a throne to do such things as are the work of a queen, to do justice between man and man, and to give to each his portion of work.

In a short time there was heard a loud shouting and the noise of a crowd of men, and Æneas perceived that a great company was coming to the temple, and when they came nearer, he saw that they were his friends from whom he had been parted by the storm. Right glad was he to see them, for he had feared very much that they had been lost. But they were all there, all, that is, except Orontes the Lycian and his crew. Æneas much wished to come forth and take them by the hand, and greet them, but he thought it better to stay where he was till he should hear their story, and see how the queen would behave to them.

Then the chief man among them, having had leave given him to speak, said: "O queen, we beseech you to receive us kindly, not to hurt our ships, and to let us dwell in peace till we can go away. Jupiter has had pity on you and allowed you to build a city; do you have pity on us. We are not come to this land to lay it waste, or to carry its spoils to our ships. There are men who do such things, but we are not of their kind. No; we have ourselves suffered too much. Our own city has been destroyed, and we are on our way to build another in the land of Italy. But as we were sailing across the sea a great storm sprang up, and scattered our ships, and those whom you now see before you are all that are left. There is no nation so savage but that it is kind to shipwrecked men. Or if there are some who are so wicked as to harm them, them the gods do not forget to punish. We had a king, Æneas by name; never was any one who better did his duty to God and man, or who was a

39

greater warrior. If he be yet alive, then we fear nothing. You will be glad to help such a man as he is. But if he is dead, then we have other friends, as King Acestes of Sicily. Give us leave therefore to lay up our ships in a safe place, to fit them with new timber from the woods, and to make new oars instead of those that have been broken by the storm. If our king and his companions are yet alive, then we will find them, and will travel with them to the land of Italy. But if he is dead and his son Ascanius also, then we go back to Sicily where there is a dwelling ready for us."

Dido said: "Be of good cheer, men of Troy. If we seemed to be unfriendly, it was because, being here in a strange land, we have to keep watch over our coasts. But now that we know who you are, we bid you welcome. Who, indeed, has not heard of Troy, and its valiant sons? Think not that we here in Carthage are so dull or so far away from the world that we do not know these things. Be sure, therefore, that whatever you are minded to do, whether to go to Italy, or to return to Sicily, we will give you all the help that you want. Or if you will settle here and dwell with us, be it so, I will make no difference between man of Troy and man of Tyre. Would that your king were here also! I will send men to seek him through all the land of Africa."

Achates said to Æneas: "Do you hear this? Our comrades are all safe; only they whom we saw drowned before our eyes are absent. Let us go forth."

While he was speaking, the cloud that was round them rolled away, and showed the two men to all the company. As for Æneas, his mother made him more beautiful to look at than he had ever been in all his life before. He stood before the queen and said: "O queen, I am the man whom you are seeking, Æneas of Troy, escaped from the waters of the sea. May the gods reward you for your kindness, because you have felt pity for all the great troubles of Troy, and because you are willing to give us, poor strangers as we are, a share in your city. So long as the rivers run to the sea, and the shadows fall among the hills, so long will your name be famous. I truly, whether I come to the land of Italy or not, shall never forget it." And he shook the hands of his friends, telling them how glad he was to be with them again.

After a while Dido spoke: "What ill fortune has brought you into such troubles? How is it that you have been driven to these savage coasts? I remember well how in the old days one Teucer came to Sidon. He had been banished from his own country, and he sought help from Belus, my grandfather. Much did he tell us about Troy and its chiefs. He praised them much, and said that he was of the same race in the beginning. Come, therefore, to my palace, and I will give you all that you want. I too have suffered much, and have wandered far. I have known many sorrows myself, and I have learnt to help them that are in trouble."

Thus the queen and all her company and Æneas and the Trojans went to the palace. There a great feast was prepared; twenty oxen and a hundred swine and a hundred sheep were made ready. And the seats for the guests were covered with purple, and the great cups of gold and silver were brought forth from the places where they were kept, and the tables were adorned with all kinds of jewels and precious things.

While these things were being done Æneas sent Achates to the ships to fetch the boy Ascanius, and to bring with him some gifts for the queen. There was a mantle, stiff with gold embroidery, which had belonged to the fair Helen. She had had it from Leda her mother. Also there was a sceptre which the eldest of the daughters of King Priam had been wont to carry, and a necklace of pearls, and a crown which had one circle of gold and another circle of precious stones.

Then they sat down to the feast; and when they had eaten enough, Dido called for a great cup from which her grandfather Belus and all the kings before him had been wont to drink, and bade them fill it to the brim. Then she said: "O Jupiter, who art the god of hosts and guests, make this day a day of joy for the men of Troy and the men of Tyre, and grant that their children may remember it for ever." When she had said this, she touched it with her lips, and handed it to Prince Bitias. He drank from it a mighty draught, and all the princes of Tyre and the Trojan chiefs did the same. After this a minstrel sang a great song about the making of men and beasts and of the stars and of the order of day and night and of the year. Also the queen asked many questions about Priam and Troy. At last she turned to Æneas and said: "Tell us now about the taking of Troy, and about the places which you have seen in your wanderings." Æneas answered: "It is a sad story, O queen, and the time is late. Nevertheless, if you will have it so, I will tell the story." So he told his story to the company.

After this Æneas and the Trojans stopped for many days in Carthage. Queen Dido loved him, and she made him her guest, and he lived in such ease and pleasure that he almost forgot all about the land of Italy, and the city which he was to build there.

But this did not please Jupiter. He said, therefore, to Mercury his messenger: "Go now and speak to Æneas these words: 'Thus speaks the king of gods and men. Is this what your mother wished when she saved you twice from the spear of the Greeks? Are you the man who is to build a city in Italy; a city which shall rule the world? If you forget these things, think of your son. Why do you take from him the kingdom that is to be his? What are you doing here? Why are you not looking to Italy? Depart at once.' "

So Mercury put his sandals on his feet, the sandals which have wings wherewith to fly, and he took his wand in his hand, and flew down from heaven. First he came to Mount Atlas, which is in the land of Africa. And from the top of Atlas he shot down, as a hawk shoots down after a bird, and came to Æneas where he stood in the middle of the city of Carthage. He had a cloak of purple, embroidered with gold, round his shoulders, and a great sword in his hand. Mercury gave him the message of Jupiter, and when he had finished it, he vanished.

For a time Æneas stood, not knowing what to do. He knew, indeed, that he was called to Italy, that he might do the will of the gods. And yet he feared to tell the thing to the queen. At last he called his chiefs together and said: "Make ready the ships, and collect the people; but do this as secretly as you may, and say nothing."

When Dido heard it—for such things are not easily hidden—she was wild with anger and love. First she came and spoke to Æneas, telling him what she had done for him and his people, and reproaching him for his ingratitude. Also she tried to keep him by telling him of the dangers of the voyage. "Stay awhile," she said, "till the stormy winds are over, and you can sail across the seas with safety." And when she could not persuade him, then she sent her sister Anna, if perhaps, he would listen to her.

But Æneas stood firm. Jupiter had bidden him go, and go he must. So, when the ships had been made ready for the voyage, he set sail, secretly and by night. And when Dido looked out from the window of her palace in the morning, lo! the ships of the Trojans were gone. Then she made up her mind that she would die. She had prepared a great pile of wood. On this she laid the sword of Æneas, which he had left behind him, and his cloak and other things which had belonged to him, and sundry possessions of her own. To this pile she set fire, and then she mounted to the top, and took the sword of Æneas in her hands, and stabbed herself with it. So she died, and the fire laid hold of the wood and made a great burning, which could be seen far off.

THE FUNERAL GAMES OF ANCHISES

Meanwhile the ships of Æneas were sailing across the sea. As they looked back to the shore which they had left they saw great flames rising up into the sky. What this meant they did not know; but they were sure that Dido was very angry, and they feared that she might do some very terrible thing.

Before long there were signs of a great storm. And Palinurus, who was the chief pilot, seeing how dark the sky had grown, said: "What do these clouds mean? What is Father Neptune going to do next?" Then he turned to Æneas and said: "We cannot get to Italy while the wind blows from this quarter; no, not even when Jupiter himself has promised it to us. Let us clear the decks, and let the men put out their oars to row, and let them shift the sails. The harbours of Sicily are near; let us make for them." Æneas answered: "You say well; let us shape our course for Sicily. There is no country which I would sooner see, for there my dear father Anchises is buried."

So they shifted their course, and let their ships run before the wind, and came in a very short time to the island of Sicily. Now Acestes, the king of the country, was the son of a Trojan woman. He had before entertained Æneas and his people very kindly, and now, when he saw their ships coming toward the land, for he happened to be standing on the top of a hill, he was very glad, and he made haste to meet them. He came to the shore, having a lion's skin about his shoulders, and carrying a spear in his hand. He greeted them with many words of kindness, and sent a supply of food and drink to the ships.

The next day, early in the morning, Æneas called all the Trojans to an assembly, and said to them: "My friends, it is a full year since we buried my dear father in this land of Sicily; yes, if I remember right, this is the very day. Let us keep it holy therefore. That, indeed, would I do, wherever I might be, whether sailing over the sea, or wandering among the lands of Africa, or even if I were shut up in some city of the Greeks. Much more, therefore, let us keep it here, seeing that we are in a friendly land, and keep it as solemnly as we can. And let us make a vow to keep it year by year in the land of Italy, if so be that we ever come to it. And now King Acestes gives us oxen for our feasts, two oxen for every ship. Therefore let us make merry and rejoice. And if the ninth day from this be fair, then we will have great games in honour of my dear father. There shall be a contest of ships, and running in a race, and games of throwing the javelin, and of shooting with the bow, and of boxing. And now make ready for the sacrifice."

First he put on his head a wreath of myrtle, for myrtle was the plant which his mother most loved. King Acestes did the same, and so did the boy Ascanius and all the Trojans. Then he came up to the tomb of his father, and poured out on it two cups of wine and two cups of pure milk, and scattered flowers over it, and said: "These gifts to thee, my father! The gods did not suffer thee to see the land of Italy, but we will do thee honour to-day."

While he was speaking a great snake came out of the tomb. Very big he was, and all the colours of the rainbow seemed to be mixed on his back. Æneas looked, wondering to see him; while he looked, the snake crept up to the altar, and tasted the sacrifice which had been put upon it, and the wine and the milk. Æneas could not think what this strange thing might mean. So he made fresh offerings, two sheep and two pigs, and two black oxen. Other Trojans also brought sheep and oxen, and sacrificed them on the tomb. And they roasted the flesh with fire—only some parts they burnt—and feasted on it.

And now the ninth day came, and the weather was fine. There came great crowds of people to see the games, for all that dwelt in the island knew the name of King Acestes. Many came to see the Trojans, and many for the sake of the games, desiring to win the prizes if they might. First the prizes were put in the midst for all to see. There were crowns of palm, and swords, and spears, and purple garments, and talents of gold and silver. And at the time that had been appointed the trumpet sounded to show that the games should begin.

First came the race of ships. Four ships there were to try for the prize. The four were the *Sea-Horse*, of which Mnestheus was the captain, the *Chimæra* of Gyas, the *Centaur* of Sergestus, and the *Scylla* of

Cloanthus. Far out to sea there was a rock. The waves beat over it when the sea was rough; but on a calm day it could be seen above the water, and the sea-birds loved to stand on it and bask in the sun. On this rock Æneas fastened a bough of an oak tree; the ships were to go round it and so home. First the captains cast lots for places. Then they took their places, each on the stern of his ship, wearing purple cloaks with gold lace upon them. The rowers had each a garland upon his head, but they were stripped for rowing, and their bodies were anointed with oil. So they sat upon the benches, with their hands stretched out, ready to dip their oars in the water for a stroke. And when the trumpet sounded the rowers dipped their oars, and rowed with all their might, and each ship leapt forward. Great was the noise of the shouting, for the people favoured this captain or that. First of all came Gyas with the *Chimæra*, and next to him Cloanthus with the *Scylla*. He had the stronger crew, but his ship was by much the heavier of the two. After these two came the *Sea-Horse* and the *Centaur*, being about equal, for now one was ahead, and now the other. When they were now near to the rock Gyas cried out to his steersman: "Why do you go so much to the right? Keep closer to the rock. Let others choose the sea if they will; I like the shortest course." But the man was afraid of rocks that could not be seen beneath the sea, and still kept the ship's head seaward. Gyas cried again: "Now make for the rock!" While he was speaking the *Scylla* came up and took the inner course between the *Chimæra* and the rock, and passed it, taking the first place. Then Gyas was so angry that he wept for very rage, and he took the steersman by the waist and threw him into the sea, and he took the rudder himself, and turned the ship to the rock. As for the steersman, being old and cumbered with his cloak, he could scarcely reach the rock. And when the people saw him thrown into the sea, and they saw how he swam to the rock, and climbed on it and sat, spitting out the salt water, they laughed. When the captains of the other two ships saw what had happened they began to hope that they too might win a prize. Mnestheus in the *Sea-Horse* seeing that the *Centaur* still kept in front of him ran among his men as they rowed—there was a plank from one end of the ship to the other—crying out: "My friends, do your best, as you have always done, whether in battle or in storms. The first place I do not seek, but I would not come back last." Then the rowers stretched out forward and threw themselves back, rowing with all their might. The *Centaur* they soon passed, for it was steered so close to the rock that it struck on a piece which jutted out, and the oars were broken and the bow stuck fast. While the crew were pushing it off with poles and the like the *Sea-Horse* got well ahead. And next it passed the *Chimæra*, for this had lost its steersman, and the captain did not know how to keep a straight course. And now only the *Scylla* was left, and the *Sea-Horse* pressed hard on it. And all the people shouted out, for it pleased them much to see that the ship which had been last was now likely to be first. Then Cloanthus, who was captain of the *Scylla*, stretched out his hands and prayed to the gods of the sea that they would help him. "Help me," he said; "help me, and I will offer a milk-white bull and much pure wine at your altar." And they heard the prayer, and one of them put out his hand, and caught hold of the keel of the ship, and sent it on, as quick as an arrow flies from the bow-string, so that it came to the shore first of the four. Then Æneas put a crown of bay-leaves about the captain's head, and gave to the rowers three oxen and jars of wine and a talent of silver. The other two also had gifts. And when Sergestus came with the *Centaur*, with half of its oars broken, just like to a serpent which the wheel of a waggon has maimed in the road, Æneas gave him a reward, for he had at least brought the ship and the crew safely back.

Next came the foot race. For this there came many, both Trojans and men of Sicily. Foremost among them all were Nisus and Euryălus, between whom there was a very close friendship. After them came Diōres, who was of the house of King Priam; after him Salius, a Greek, and two young hunters, who were of the court of King Acestes, and many others. Æneas said: "I will give gifts to all who run; none shall go away empty. To the first three I will give crowns of olive. The first also shall have a horse with its trappings; the second a quiver full of arrows, and a belt with which to fasten it; the third must be content with a Greek helmet."

Then all the men stood in a line, and when the signal was given they started. For a short time they were all close together. Then Nisus outran the rest. Next to him came Salius, but there was a long space between them; and next to Salius was Euryălus. The fourth was one of the king's courtiers, Helymus by name, and close behind him the Trojan Diōres. When they had nearly come to the end of the course, by bad luck Nisus slipped in the blood of an ox which had been slain in the place, and fell. But as he lay on the ground he did not forget his friend Euryălus, for he lifted himself from the ground just as Salius came running in, and tripped him up. So Euryălus had the first place, Helymus was second, and Diōres third. But Salius loudly complained that he had been cheated. "I had won the first prize," he cried, "had not this Nisus tripped me up." But the people favoured Euryălus, for he was a comely lad; Diōres also was on the same side, for otherwise he had not won the third prize. "Then," said Æneas, "I will not change the order; let them take the prizes as they come—Euryălus the first, Helymus the second, and Diōres the third. Nevertheless I will have pity on the man who suffered not from his own fault." And he gave to Salius a lion's skin, of which the mane and the claws were covered with gold. Then Nisus said: "If you are giving prizes to these who are beaten, then think of me, for I was first, and slipped, having the same bad luck of which Salius complains." And he showed his face and body all covered with filth. And Æneas laughed and gave him a noble shield.

After this came the boxing match. The winner's prize was an ox with gilded horns, the loser would have a sword and a helmet. Immediately Dares stood up; he was a giant in height and breadth. He was the only man who had ever dared to meet Paris, the strongest boxer in Troy; he had also vanquished a famous champion, Butes by name, hurting him so that he died of his wounds. So mighty a man did he seem that no one had the courage to stand up against him. So Dares came to Æneas where he sat, and said: "If there is no man to meet me let me take the prize." But King Acestes said to his friend Entellus, who was sitting next to him on the grass: "Entellus, will you suffer this prize to be taken in this fashion? Did you not learn this art from Eryx himself? Has not your fame gone through this land of Sicily? Is not your house full of prizes that you have won?" Entellus answered: "Think not, O king, that I am afraid, or that I do not care for honour; but I am old, and I have lost my strength. If I had been as young as that boaster there I should not have wanted a prize to make me go and meet this bragging fellow."

Then he stood up and threw onto the ground two boxing gloves which the great boxer Eryx had used of old. All who saw them were astonished, so big were they, heavy with bull's hide and lumps of lead and iron. As for Dares, he said: "I will not stand up against such as these." And when Æneas took them up, trying their weight, Entellus said: "What would this Trojan have thought if he had seen the gloves which Hercules wore when he fought with this same Eryx and killed him? These Eryx himself—he, O Æneas! was your mother's son—gave me. See the marks of blood and brains upon them! These are of the men who fought with him. But if Dares likes them not, be it so; I will put them away, and he shall put away his."

Then he threw off the cloak which he wore, and showed his shoulders and arms, how big and strong they were.

Then Æneas gave to each gloves of equal weight, and the two stood and faced each other. Dares was more nimble and quick, for he was young; Entellus, though a giant in height and breadth, was slow and scant of breath. Many blows they aimed at each other, and sometimes one would strike the other on the breast or the cheek, but neither struck home. Entellus stood in the same place, swaying one way and the other, with eyes always watching his enemy. As for Dares, he was like a general who attacks a city, and tries first one part and then another, if he can find the weakest. At last Entellus, thinking that he could reach the other, dealt him a great blow; but Dares, seeing it coming, leapt out of the way; and the old man wasted his strength in the air, and fell with a crash, as a pine tree falls on the side of a hill. All the men of Troy and the men of Sicily ran up to see what had happened; and Acestes ran, and would have helped the old man to rise. But he got up of himself, for shame and anger, as it were, made him young again. Dares fled before him, and Entellus followed him over the plain, hitting him, now with the right hand, and now with the left; and the blows were like hail when it rattles on a roof. Then Æneas cried: "Be not angry, my friend;" and to Dares he said: "See you not that the gods are against you to-day? Do not fight against the gods." So he commanded that the battle should cease. Dares was led away by his friends in sad plight, spitting out blood, yea, and his teeth, for they were broken in the fight. And they took with them the shield and the helmet; but the crown of palms and the ox they left to Entellus. And he said: "See, Æneas and you men of Troy, what I could do when I was young." And he lifted up his hand, and struck the ox between the brows. And the beast fell dead upon the ground. And the old man said: "Eryx, take this offering. I give you this ox instead of the life of Dares: and, indeed, it is the better thing of the two. And here I lay down my gloves for ever."

Next to this came the trial of shooting with the bow. Æneas set up the mast of a ship, and to the top of the mast he tied a dove by a cord. This was the mark at which all were to shoot. The first hit the mast, and shook it, and all could see how the bird fluttered his wings. Then the second shot. He did not touch the bird, but he cut the string by which it was fastened to the mast, and the bird flew away. Then the third, a man of Lycia, aimed at the bird itself, and struck it as it flew, and the dove fell dead to the earth with the arrow through it. Last of all, King Acestes shot his arrow. And he, having nothing at which to aim, shot it high into the air, to show how strong a bow he had and how he could draw it. Then there happened a strange thing to see. The arrow, as it went higher and higher in the air, was seen to catch fire, and to leave a line of flame behind it, till it was burnt up. When Æneas saw this, he said to himself: "This is a sign of good to come," for he thought how the fire had burnt on the head of his son Ascanius, and how a star had shot through the air when he was about to fly from Troy. And as this had been a sign of good at the beginning of his wanderings, so was this a sign of good at the end. Then he threw his arms about King Acestes, saying: "I thank thee, my father. This is a message which Jupiter sends by you." And he gave him a great bowl of silver which his father Anchises had had before him. The other archers also had gifts according to the skill which they had shown.

Last of all, there was a new game which none had seen before. Ascanius and his young companions came riding on horses, three companies of twelve each with a leader. They had crowns on their heads, and collars of gold on their necks, and carried spears in their hands. They rode this way and that way, making a show of fighting. Sometimes they seemed to charge, and sometimes to fly. And all the people shouted, so fair were the lads, and so well did they ride.

THE BURNING OF THE SHIPS—THE COMING TO ITALY

While the Trojans were busy with the games, Juno was busy doing them a great mischief, for she saw that they were now very near to the end of their wanderings, that is to say, the land of Italy. And the mischief was this, to burn their ships.

The women sat by themselves near the ships, making a great wailing for Anchises. And as they looked at the sea they thought to themselves: "Surely we have travelled enough; surely we have had enough of the sea: would it not be far better that we should have a city in which to dwell?"

Now Juno had sent down her messenger Iris to do this business for her. So when Iris knew what the women were thinking, she took the shape of a Trojan woman, Beroë by name, and went among them and said: "Surely, my sisters, it would have been better for us if we had been killed by the Greeks when they took the city of Troy. Seven summers have come and gone since we left our native country, and we are still wandering over sea and land. We seek this land of Italy, but it seems to be always flying before us, and we never see it. Here we have friends and kinsfolk. Why should we not build here a city? Why should we not burn these accursed ships which carry us hither and thither? Last night I saw in a dream the prophetess Cassandra. She seemed to say to me: 'Here is Troy; here is the home for which you are seeking.' And as she said this, she put a torch in my hand. See now the altars here, and the fire upon them." And she caught a torch from the altar, and threw it at the ships.

But another woman, who had been nurse to the sons of King Priam, cried out: "Women of Troy, this is not Beroë who is speaking to you. Beroë I left just now, very sick and much vexed that she could not come to this our meeting here. No; this is not Beroë. Look how she walks, and what shining eyes she has." The women stood in doubt, not knowing what to do. They would have liked to stay where they were, and yet they knew that they were called to the land of Italy. But while they doubted, they saw Iris going up to heaven by the path of the rainbow, and they cried out: "It is a goddess who has spoken to us!" And a great rage came upon them; every one of them caught up a torch from the altars, and ran and set fire to the ships. In a moment the flames ran over the benches and the oars and the stems of pine. Some one ran at once to the Trojans as they sat looking at the games, and told them what was going on: they themselves, too, saw a great cloud of smoke coming up from the sea. Ascanius heard of the matter while he was leading his host, and immediately he galloped down to the shore. When he got to the ships, he cried out: "What are you doing? This is not the camp of the Greeks that you are burning. You are burning your own hopes. See, I am your own Ascanius." And he took his helmet from his head, and stood bareheaded before them. After him came Æneas and the other Trojans, as fast as they could. And when the women thought of what they had done, they were much ashamed of their behaviour, and sought to hide themselves. But not the less did the fire burn the ships, nor could the Trojans, when they tried to put it out, do any good. Then Æneas rent his garments and cried out: "O Jupiter, if thou carest for us at all, save our ships, lest we perish altogether. But if thou art angry, and if I have done wrong, slay me with thy thunderbolt, but save my people."

While he was still speaking, a great storm came up from the south, with thunder and lightning and a great rain. So the fire was put down. Nevertheless, four of the ships were burnt entirely.

Æneas was much troubled at these things, and thought in himself what he had better do. Should he stay in Sicily, where he had friends?—for though the Fates called him to Italy, yet there was ever something to hinder his going. Then a certain priest, a wise man, one who knew better than all others the mind of the gods, said to him: "Surely we must go to the place whither the gods call us. That it is not lawful to doubt. Nevertheless, you may think of something that shall help us in our present need. I would have you ask advice from King Acestes, for he is your friend, and not only so, but of the same race as we are. See now; four ships have been burnt, and there are too many people here for such as are left. And see again; some do not like the thing which you purpose to do. There are old men and women who are weary of the sea; there are some that are weak; and there are some whose courage fails them. Let King Acestes, if he will, take these for himself. Let him build a city for them, and call it Acesta after his own name." But before he could do anything in the matter the night came, and Æneas went to his bed. While he slept he saw his father in a dream. The old man said: "My son, Jupiter has sent me to you. Take the advice which has been given you, for it is good. Choose out the best and strongest of your people to go with you, for you will have to do with a strong and fierce people in this land of Italy to which you go. But first come and see me in the place where I dwell below the earth. The Sibyl, whose abode is in Cumæ, will show you the way; there you shall hear all that shall come to you and to your children after. And now I must go, for the morning is coming."

So Æneas took counsel with the chief of the Trojans, and with King Acestes. And the king was willing to do the thing that Æneas asked of him. So they made a division of the people. Those that were strong and brave were to go with Æneas, and those who were weak and doubtful and faint-hearted were to stay. So Æneas marked out the boundaries of the city with a plough, and King Acestes set everything in order.

On the ninth day, after much feasting, Æneas and his men departed, not without many tears from those who were going and those who were left behind. And when the south wind blew softly, they set sail; and the god of the sea gave them a smooth passage. So they came to the land of Italy, to Cumæ, the dwelling of the Sibyl. The men pushed the ships on to the beach, turning their foreparts to the sea, and making them fast with anchors and ropes. While they were busy with this Æneas went up to the temple. It was a wonderful place which Dædălus himself had built when he came to Italy from the island of Crete. For Dædălus had made wings for himself and for Icarus his son, and so had fled from Crete when King Minos would have killed him. He himself came safe, but his son, flying too high in the air, had the wax melted from his wings, and so fell into the sea and was drowned. And Dædălus had set forth all the story of the things that had happened in Crete, carving all the figures in stone. Only when he came to set forth the death of his son, his heart failed him, so great was his grief.

Then the Sibyl, who was a prophetess, told Æneas something of what should happen to him in the land of Italy. And when he had heard her prophecy, he said: "O Lady, I have something more to ask of you. My father, Anchises, has bidden me, not once or twice, but many times, to go down to the place where he dwells among the dead. Will you, therefore, be my guide, for you know the way?"

The Sibyl said: "It is easy to go down to the dwellings of the dead, but it is hard to come back. Nevertheless, if it is lawful for you to go, then I will go with you. And this is how you may know whether it is lawful. There is in the very middle of a wood hard by a tree on which there grows a bough of gold. If you can find this bough, and if, when you have found it, you are able to pluck it from its place, then you may know that it is lawful for you to go."

So Æneas went into the wood, and the doves of his mother went before him, guiding him to the place where the golden bough was growing. And when he saw it, he put out his hand, and plucked it, and it came off at once. Then he went back to the Sibyl, and the two went together. Now the things which they saw are told elsewhere. It will be sufficient to say in this place, that Æneas found his father in the happy place which they called the Elysian Fields. Very glad were they to meet again. And Anchises showed his son a long line of his descendants who should be in the time to come. There were the kings of Alba, and Romulus, who should build the great city of Rome, and Brutus, who should set that city free when tyrants were ruling over it, and wise men who should make laws, and soldiers who should win great victories—a most noble company. "See," he said, "your children's children. Others shall carve the face of men in marble, or mold it in bronze more skilfully; others shall be more eloquent in speech, and know better the rising and setting of the stars. It is the work of your children's children to rule the world."

So Æneas, when he had seen and heard these things, went up again to the world above.

IN ITALY

While Æneas and his people were at Cumæ, Caiëta his old nurse, who had gone with him in all his wanderings, died. He called a great cliff that there was close by after her name, and it is so called to this day. After this they set sail, the south wind blowing softly and carrying them on to the place which they sought. As they went, they passed by the island where Circé lived—Circé, who was said to be a daughter of the Sun, and who was a great witch. She used to sit all day and weave on her loom wonderful work with pictures on it, and as she sat she sang with a very sweet voice. And if any traveller went in to see who it was that sang so sweetly, she would give him a cup of wine. But this wine was poisoned, and when the man had drunk it, Circé would wave a wand over his head, and he became a beast—a lion, or a bear, or a wolf, or, it may be, a pig. The Trojans, as they sailed by, heard these creatures growling or roaring. But Neptune made the wind blow more strongly, so that they passed very quickly by, for he was afraid that they might come to some harm.

After a little time they came to a place where there was a great wood along the shore, and in the midst of the wood a river, the name of which was the Tiber. This was the place where it flowed into the sea. And they saw that the water of the river was very yellow. It has always been called the "Yellow Tiber." Here they brought their ships to land. And Æneas and his son Ascanius and some of the princes got out on to the shore and sat down under one of the trees to have their dinner. They made plates of dough, and on these they put such fruits as they could find. It was but a scanty meal, and when they had eaten all the fruits they were still hungry. Then they began to break up their platters of dough and to eat them. And the boy Ascanius said, laughing: "What! do we even eat our tables?" When Æneas heard these words, he was very glad, and he caught the boy in his arms and kissed him, saying, "Now this is a good word that you have said, my son! Long ago that dreadful creature the Harpy said that some day we should be so pressed by hunger that we should eat our tables. My father also prophesied that when we did this we might know that we had indeed come to the land where we were to have a home. And now this has come to pass. This is our home, and as for the hunger which I feared, lo! we have endured it and are yet alive!" Then the chiefs told the story to all the people, and all rejoiced together.

And now it must be told what this country was to which they had come. The name of it was Latium, and the name of the king was Latinus. He was the son of Faunus, who was the son of Picus, and Picus was the son of Saturn. The story that was told about Saturn was this, that when his son Jupiter turned him out of his throne in heaven, for he had been king of gods and men, he fled away to Italy, and set up a kingdom there, and reigned in great peace and happiness. Now King Latinus had no son, but only a daughter, Lavinia by name, who was now of an age to be married. Many chiefs of Italy desired to have her for a wife, but the one whom the queen her mother liked beyond all the others was a certain Turnus. He was a very tall and handsome young man, and a great soldier, and was also the son of a king. Nor was King Latinus himself unwilling that Turnus should be his son-in-law, but the wise men, the priests and the prophets, told him that it must not be, because the gods would not have it so. And one of the signs by which the prophets knew that this was so, was this. There was in the middle of the palace a great bay tree. It was growing there when the king built the palace; and he made it sacred to the god Apollo and built an altar under its branches. One day a swarm of bees came flying into the court where the bay tree was, and settled on it, and hung down from one of the branches, in the shape of a cluster, as is the way of bees when they swarm. Then the prophets said: "As the bees have come to your palace, O king, so there shall come a strange people from far away to this land, and their king shall be the husband of your daughter." Not many days after this as Lavinia was standing by her father's side, and lighted the fire on the altar, a flame leapt from the altar on to her hair, and burnt the ornaments that she wore on her head, and spread with much smoke, and fire over the whole palace. But the girl herself was not burnt. The prophets, when they knew this, said: "This maiden shall be famous and great; but a dreadful war shall come upon her people, and many shall perish." Then the king himself, wishing to know for certain what he ought to do, went to a temple that was near to his palace, being the temple of his father Faunus. Of this temple he was himself the priest. The custom was that if the priest wished to inquire of the god, he sacrificed sheep, and lay down to sleep on their skins. This the king did. He made a sacrifice of a hundred sheep, and lay down to sleep upon the skins. And lo! before he fell asleep there came a voice from out the inner part of the temple: "My son, seek not to marry thy daughter to a prince of this land. There shall come a son-in-law from over the sea. Give thy daughter to him. He shall make this land to be the greatest under the whole heaven." The king did not keep this to himself, but told it to every one.

It came to pass, therefore, that Æneas, asking questions of some people of the country whom he met on the day after his coming, heard about these things. So he said to himself: "I will send an embassy to this King Latinus, and beg of him that there may be peace between his people and my people. But lest by chance either he or any one of the princes hereabouts should seek to do us harm, I will provide a place of defence." So he chose a hundred men who should be ambassadors for him, and put crowns of olive on their heads, and sent them with gifts in their hands to the king. When these had set out, he marked out a place for a camp, and he commanded the people to work as hard as they could, making it strong with a mound and a ditch.

The ambassadors, going on their way to the city, came to a great plain where the young men of the place were amusing themselves with contests and games. Some raced against each other, riding on horses or driving chariots. Some shot with bows and arrows; others threw javelins, or ran races on foot, or boxed or wrestled. As soon as the Trojans were seen, one of the horsemen rode as fast as he could to the city, and told the king, saying: "Some men in strange clothes have come, desiring to see you." Latinus said: "Bring them before me." And he put on his king's robes, and sat on his throne.

A very noble place was the king's palace. Picus had built it on a hill in the middle of the city, with a sacred wood all round it. It had a hundred pillars, fifty on one side and fifty on the other; among the pillars were statues of kings of old time. On the walls were hung spoils taken in war, battle-axes, and spears, and helmets, and the beaks of ships, and the yokes of chariots. In this hall the kings of the country of Latium were crowned; and the princes met in it to take counsel together, and great feasts were held in it.

King Latinus said: "Men of Troy, for, indeed, I know who you are, tell me why you have come to this land. Are you seeking something, or have you come by chance? Have storms driven you out of your course?—for this, I know, is a thing which often happens to men who sail over the sea. Be sure that, whatever be the cause of your coming, you are welcome. In this land we walk in the way of the good King Saturn, and do the thing that is right, not by constraint but of our own will. Know also that we are of the same blood, for Dardănus, who was the first founder of Troy, came from a certain city in this land."

Then the chief of the ambassadors answered: "O king, we have not wandered out of our way, nor have storms driven us upon this coast. We have come hither on purpose. I doubt not, O king, that you know how we were driven out of our own country. Who, indeed, is there on the whole face of the earth who does not know what a great destroying storm came out from the land of Greece and laid the great city of Troy even with the ground? What we ask of you, O king, is a parcel of ground on which we may build a city to dwell in; also that we may breathe the air and drink the water of this land. Be sure, O king, that we shall do no harm to this thy country, and that you will not be sorry for having received us. Of a truth, many nations have desired that we should join ourselves to them. But the gods laid a command upon us that we should come to this land of Italy. For, as you have yourself said, it was from this land that Dardănus, our first father, came forth, and hither, by the will of the gods, his children's children must come back. So we heard from Apollo himself. And now we pray you, O king, to receive these gifts which our lord Æneas sends by our hands. This is the sceptre which King Priam was used to hold in his hand when he did justice among his people. These garments the ladies of Troy worked with their own hands."

For a while the king sat silent, thinking over these things in his heart. For he said to himself: "Is this man whom they call Æneas, he of whom my father Faunus spoke? Is he, perchance, the son-in-law who, the prophets said, should come from some strange land to be the husband of my daughter Lavinia?" At the last he spoke, saying: "May the gods grant that there be peace and friendship between us and you. We grant, men of Troy, the things for which you ask—a parcel of ground, and air and water. We also thank your king for his gifts. Be sure that in this land there are such riches as shall match even the riches of Troy. As for your king, Æneas, if he wishes to be our friend, let him come and look upon us, face to face. Take also this message to him: 'I have a daughter, whom the gods forbid me to marry to any prince of this land. For they say that there shall come a stranger from over the sea to be my son-in-law, and that from him shall come a race which shall raise the name of Italy even to the stars of heaven.' "

Then Latinus said to his people: "Bring forth horses for these men." Now there stood in the king's stable three hundred horses, the swiftest of their kind: of these the servants brought forth a hundred, one for every Trojan. All of them had trappings of purple and bits of gold. To Æneas himself the king sent a chariot drawn by two horses, which were of the breed of the horses of the Sun. So the ambassadors went back to the camp with noble gifts and a message of peace.

THE PLOTS OF JUNO

When Juno saw that the Trojans were come to the land of Italy, and that they were building houses in which to dwell, and that King Latinus was showing them no little kindness, she said to herself: "So this wicked race has vanquished me. The flames of the burning city of Troy did not destroy them, nor did the sea swallow them up. And lo! they have come unharmed to the river Tiber, to the very place which they desired. Yes: it is but too true; I, who am the sister and the wife of Jupiter, have been overcome by this Æneas. Nevertheless there is still something which I can do. The gods in heaven will not help me; therefore I will go to the powers of hell. I cannot keep this fellow from the kingdom of Latium, and it is the pleasure of the gods that he should have Lavinia for his wife. But I will see to it that he shall buy this kingdom of his at a great price, and that your dowry, O daughter of Latinus, shall be the blood of Italy and of Troy. Then Juno went down into the lower parts of the earth, and called to her Alecto, who was one of the Furies, who loved anger and war and treachery, and all evil and hateful things. Even her own sisters, the Furies, could not bear to look on her, so dreadful was she to behold. Juno said to her: "Daughter of Night, I have suffered a great wrong and disgrace, and I want you to help me. A man whom I hate, Æneas by name, desires to have a kingdom in Italy: keep him from it. He wishes to have Lavinia, the daughter of King Latinus, to wife: see that he does not. You can set brother against brother; you can bring strife into kingdoms and into homes. Break this peace that the Latins and the Trojans are making. Bring about some occasion of war."

Alecto first went to the palace of Latinus. There she found the queen, Amata by name, in great anger and trouble. She was much displeased by the doings of the king, her husband. She did not wish to have Æneas for her son-in-law, and she loved the prince Turnus with all her heart. Then the Fury thought to herself: "The queen hates

Æneas already; I will turn her hatred into madness." So she took a snake out of her hair and thrust it into the bosom of the queen. The evil beast crept about her so that the poison got into her heart; then it changed itself into a collar, as of twisted gold, round her neck, and poisoned her very breath.

At the first, before the evil altogether overpowered her, she spoke gently to her husband, weeping as a mother might weep when she is afraid that she may lose her daughter. She said: "Are you not afraid, my husband, to give Lavinia to this exile from Troy? Have you no pity for her or me or yourself? Well I know that so soon as the north wind begins to blow, he will fly from this land and carry her away with him. Do you not care for the promise that you made to Turnus—yes, made with an oath—that he should have Lavinia for his wife? You say that she must marry a stranger. Is he not a stranger? Are not all who are not subjects of your kingdom strangers? This, and this only, is what the gods command. Further, if you look into the matter, you will see that he is a stranger also in race, for he is of the family of Inachus, and is by race a Greek."

But when she saw that her husband was not moved at all by her words, the madness altogether overcame her. She rushed out of the palace, and through the streets of the city, taking her daughter with her. And, as she went, she called to the other women to follow her, so that a whole multitude went after her. Like to so many wild creatures, they ran through the woods, the queen leading them, holding a burning torch in her hand, and singing the marriage song of her daughter and Turnus.

The next thing that the Fury did was that she went to the city where Turnus lived. He was asleep, and the Fury went in and stood by his bedside. She had taken the shape of an old woman, the priestess of the Temple of Juno, and she said: "Turnus, are you content that you should lose that which is your right, and that your kingdom should be taken from you? King Latinus takes from you the wife that he had promised, and is about to hand over his kingdom to a stranger from over the sea. Juno bade me come and tell you this. Arm your people; drive these strangers out of the land, and burn their ships with fire. And if the king will not keep his promise, let him learn for himself that Turnus is not one who will suffer wrong."

So the old woman spoke, and Turnus answered—for so it seemed to him in his dream—"Old woman, I know that the ships of the strangers have come to the Tiber. But these are idle tales that you tell me. I know that Queen Juno cares for me; therefore, I am not afraid. But you, mother, are old, and wander somewhat in your wits, and trouble yourself for nothing, and are afraid when there is nothing to fear. Keep, I pray you, to your own business; serve the temples of the gods, but leave war and the things of war to men, for such matters belong to them."

And then it seemed to Turnus in his dream that the old woman grew very angry, yea, that she changed into the shape of a Fury, and that a thousand snakes hissed round her. And when he tried to speak again, the words would not come, and when he would have risen from his bed, she thrust him back, and caught two snakes from her hair and lashed him with them, crying: "I am old, forsooth! and I wander from my wits! and I am afraid when I have nothing to fear! Nay, but I am the greatest of the Furies, and war and death are in my hands." And it seemed to him, still in his dream, that she threw a lighted torch at him, and that it fixed itself in his heart. Then he woke with a great start. He did not know whether the things which he had seen and heard in his sleep were true or not, but his heart was full of anger. He called for his arms, and commanded all the young men to make themselves ready for war. "I will drive these Trojans," he cried, "out of Italy, and if Latinus and his people stand by them, then they shall go also."

And now there was one thing left for the Fury to do, and this was to make a cause of quarrel. King Latinus had a man to keep his cattle, and this man's daughter, Silvia by name, had a tame stag which her brothers had found when it was a fawn, and had brought to her. The girl was very fond of the creature, and would put garlands of flowers about its neck, and comb its hair, and give it a bath. All day long the stag would wander about the woods, and at night it came back to the house. Now it so happened that Ascanius, with other Trojan lads, was hunting that day, and his dogs caught scent of the stag and followed it. And Ascanius, riding after them, saw the beast, and shot an arrow at it, and hit it, for the Fury took care that the arrow should not miss its aim. Then the stag, being wounded to death, ran back to the herdsman's house, and filled it with most lamentable cries. Silvia heard it, and was greatly grieved to see her dear pet in such a case, and cried out for help. And here again the

Fury—for she was hiding in the woods—did all she could to increase the trouble. From all sides the country folk came together, each picking up for a weapon anything that came to hand. One had a brand that had been half-burned in the fire, and another a great stick with knots in it. The herdsman himself carried an axe in his hand. On the other hand, the Trojans ran together to help Ascanius, and soon there was a regular battle. Some were slain both on the one side and on the other. Among them was Almo, who was the eldest son of the herdsman, and an old man Galæsus, who was killed as he tried to make peace between the two parties. He came between them as they fought, and the spears wounded him to the death. A good man was he, and rich, for he had five flocks of sheep and five herds of cattle, and as much land for wheat and the like as could be worked by a hundred ploughs.

Then said Juno to the Fury: "It is enough; go to your own place. Jupiter would be angry if he saw you here. The rest I will do."

THE GATHERING OF THE CHIEFS

When the battle was over—for the Trojans, being more used to war, soon drove the Latins back—the shepherds carried the two dead men, Almo and Galæsus, to the city, and cried for vengeance to the gods and to the king. And none cried louder and more fiercely than Turnus: "Why," said he, "do you put the Trojans before me?" And all the people said the same thing, crying out: "Send away these Trojans. Let us have our own people to rule over us." As for the king, he stood firm, firm as a great rock in the sea. The waves break over it, and the sea-weed is dashed against it, but it is not heaved from its place. At last he said: "O foolish Latins, you will pay for this madness with your lives; and no one, O Turnus, will suffer worse things than you; and when you would cry to the gods for help, they will not hear you. As for me, I shall soon be at rest in the grave. And if I have but little honour at my funeral, what matters it?"

There was a custom of old time in Latium, and in Alba afterwards, and in Rome herself in later times, that when there is the beginning of war, they open the great gate of the Temple of Janus. When the Fathers have given their voice for war, then the consul himself, in robe and girdle, opens the gate with his own hand, and the people follow him, and there is a great blowing of horns. But King Latinus, though the people bade him declare war and open the gate, would have nothing to do with it; he hid himself. So Juno herself came down, and opened the gate with her own hand.

When this had been done, men made ready for battle throughout all the land of Italy. They polished their shields, and sharpened their spears and swords and battle-axes. In five cities forges were set up, wherein to make new arms and armour, helmets and shields, and breastplates and greaves. Even their ploughs and their reaping-hooks they took and turned them into weapons of war.

First came King Mezentius, the Tuscan, of whom more will soon be said. He was one who cared not for gods or men. With him came Lausus his son; there was no fairer or better youth in Italy. He deserved to have a better father. With these two came a thousand men.

Next came a son of Hercules, carrying a shield on which was his father's crest, the great monster with a hundred heads, which men called the Hydra. He had a lion's skin, with a mane and great white teeth round his head and shoulders. He was followed by the Sabines, who were armed with long spears and swords.

After him came the twin brothers who built the city of Tibur. They were Greeks, and with them came a son of Vulcan, and a great company of country folk, some of them carrying slings and some javelins. These had helmets of wolf-skin on their heads.

Next came Messāpus, skilled in taming horses, the son of Neptune. His father had given him charms which made him safe against fire and sword. Many other chiefs of great renown followed, all with companies of men. Some had wicker shields and some helmets made of cork, and others spears and shields of bronze, for in old time men used bronze and not iron for making of arms and armour. Their names need not be told in this place; only Umbro the priest. A wise man was he, and one who could charm serpents and heal those who were bitten by them. But he could not heal the wound of the Trojan spear, nor did all his charms keep him from death.

But of all that came there was none more brave, or strong, or fair to look upon than Turnus, for as he stood in the midst he overtopped all others by the head. He had a helmet on his head, and on the helmet three crests, with the Chimæra, a creature of which half was a lion and half a goat. A great multitude of men followed him.

Last of all came Camilla, a wonderful girl from the land of the Volscians. And with her came a great company of women warriors, with armour of bronze, and riding on horses. This Camilla cared not for the distaff, or to spin, or to do such things as women are used to do. She cared for nothing but war. A great fighter was she, and also a wonderful runner. She was swifter than the winds. She could run over the standing corn, and not break it down; she could run across the sea, and not wet her feet. All the young men were astonished to see her, and the women looked after her, as she went. She had a purple mantle round her shoulders, and a band of gold round her hair; on her back she carried a quiver of arrows and a bow, and in her hand she had a pike of myrtle-wood.

KING EVANDER

When Æneas heard that the nations of Italy were gathering together against him and that they had sent an embassy to Diomed, who was the bravest of the Greeks after Achilles, he was much troubled. He knew that he and his Trojans were but few against many, and he did not know where to look for help. While he was thinking about these things, he fell asleep. In his dreams the god of the river, Father Tiber, as he was called, appeared to him. He was an old man, with a garment of blue linen, and a crown of reeds on his head. The old man said to him—so it seemed to Æneas in his dream—"You are welcome to this land, you and the gods of Troy whom you bring with you. Do not be troubled by wars and rumours of wars, nor give up the work which you have begun. It is the will of the gods that this shall prosper in the end. And now you are looking for help; I will tell you, therefore, where you will find it. Certain men from the land of Arcadia came to this country of Italy, with their king, Evander, and have built a city which they call Pallantēum. These men are always at war with the Latins. Go to them, therefore, and make a treaty with them that their enemies shall be your enemies and their friends your friends. And the way by which you must go is my stream; for know that I am Father Tiber, and that of all the rivers under the sun there is none that is dearer to the gods than mine. Rise, therefore, and worship the gods, especially Queen Juno, that she may cease to hate you."

When Æneas woke out of sleep, he remembered that, long before, the prophet Helenus had said to him that when he was in great need of help it should come to him against all hope—that is to say, from a city of the Greeks. Then he took enough of his people to fill two ships, and went his way. And those that were left worked as hard as they could making the walls of the camp strong and the ditch deep.

By noon they had travelled some twenty miles, for Father Tiber had made their work easy, staying his stream so that they might find it more easy to row. So they came to a place where there were seven hills, and a citadel on one of them, and some houses scattered about. This was the city of Evander.

It so happened that the king and his people had sacrificed that day to Hercules, as they used to do every year, and were sitting at the feast afterwards. When they saw the ships through the trees, they were a little troubled. They feared that the strangers might be enemies, for, indeed, they had but few friends in the country. So they all jumped up from their places. But the King's son, whose name was Pallas, cried out: "Sit still: do not disturb the feast: as for these strangers, I will look to them." So he snatched up a spear, and, standing on the little hill on which the altar had been built, he cried: "Strangers, why have you come to this place? What do you want? Do you bring peace or war?"

Æneas, who was standing on the stern of his ship, holding an olive branch in his hand—this was a sign of peace—cried with a loud voice: "We are men of Troy; the Latins are our enemies; we are seeking King Evander. Say to the king, if you will, that Æneas, prince of Troy, has come, and wishes to make alliance with him."

Now Pallas had heard the name of Æneas, and that he was a great chief; but more he did not know. He answered: "Come near, whoever you are; I will take you to my father, the king." So Æneas stepped on to the shore, and Pallas brought him to the king.

Æneas said: "I have come to you, O King, of my own accord: I am not afraid of you, though I know that you are a Greek, and not only that, but a kinsman of the two sons of Atreus, the very men who destroyed my city of Troy. For you are my kinsman also. We are both of us of the race of Atlas. And there is this also between you and me: we are both of us strangers in this land, and the people of it hate us both. And I am very sure that if they overcome me they will also overcome you. So there will be no one who can stand against them. They will rule over Italy from sea to sea. Therefore I have to ask for your help, and to give help to you. I would not send ambassadors—I have come myself. It is thus that men become most quickly friends."

As Æneas was speaking, the king never took his eyes off him. And when he had finished, he caught him by the hand, and said: "Welcome, great son of Troy! I seem myself to see the face and hear the voice of Anchises. Well I remember how Priam came long ago to see his sister, who was the wife of Telamon; and with him came Anchises, with other princes of Troy; but there was not one of them who could be compared with Anchises. When he went away, he gave me a bow made in Lycia, and a quiver full of arrows, also a cloak embroidered with gold, and two bridles of gold which Pallas my son has to this day. The help which you ask I will give; my people are as your people. To-morrow, if you will, you shall go, and take with you as many men as I can find for you. But now, for you are come on a good day, sit down and join us at our feast."

So Æneas sat down by the king's side, and all the Trojans had seats at the feast, and they ate, and drank, and were merry. When they had had enough to eat and drink, King Evander said: "We keep this day to Hercules, and with good reason." And he told him

THE STORY OF CACUS

"Hercules, as you have doubtless heard, came into these parts to fetch the cattle of Gēryon. The cattle were strange creatures, for they were red, red as is the sky at sunset; and their master was strange, for he had three bodies; and the keepers of the herd were strange also, a great giant and a dog with two heads. All these terrible creatures Hercules killed, and drove away the cattle, bringing them back to the master whom he served, who dwelt in the land of Greece. In his journey he came to this place. At that time there was living in a cave close by a famous robber, Cacus by name. He was the son, men said, of Vulcan, the god of fire, and so was able to breathe out fire from his mouth. All men were afraid of him, for who could fight with a man that could scorch his adversary by breathing fire upon him? Hercules then lay down to sleep under a tree, and the cattle grazed all about the bank of the river. When Cacus saw them, and saw that for shape and colour they were such that no other cattle in the world could be compared with them, he took four bulls and four heifers, the very finest that there were in the whole herd. These he dragged by their tails to his cave, that it might not be seen where they were, for the marks of their hoofs seemed to be going away from the cave, not to it, and he rolled a great stone to the mouth of the cave. The next day, as Hercules was about to go on his journey, the bulls and the heifers which were in the cave, knowing that their companions were going away, and not liking to be left behind, set up a great lowing. When Hercules heard this he knew that he had been robbed, not having known it before because the herd was very great; and he was full of anger. He took up his great club, and climbed to the top of the hill which covered the cave. Cacus saw him coming, and fled as fast as he could to his cave. For the first time in his life he was afraid, for he saw that this stranger was far stronger and fiercer than any man that he had ever seen before. So he ran as fast as he could to his cave, and made a great block of stone which was hanging over the door drop down. It had been made so cleverly that it seemed exactly like the rest of the side of the mountain. Hercules knew that the cattle were inside the mountain, for he still could hear them lowing, but where the door of the cave might be he could not tell. He went from place to place, gnashing his teeth in his rage. Three times he tried to pull away the rock, and each time he found that it was part of the solid side of the mountain. At last he saw on the top a great piece of stone jutting out, which seemed to lean toward the river. So he went and pushed against this with all his strength—and there was not so strong a man in all the earth—and at last it gave way, and the whole side of the mountain fell with it into the river beneath. Then the cave of Cacus could be seen, so horrible a place as had never been shown before to the eyes of men. And in the depth of the cave was the monster himself. Hercules took the bow which he carried on his shoulders and arrows from his quiver—such arrows as no man but he possessed—but he could not hit the monster, for the cave was filled with fire and smoke which Cacus poured out of his mouth. But Hercules was not to be put off in this way. He plunged into the cave, and groped about till in the place where the smoke was thickest he found the creature. He caught him in his arms, and struck him with his club, and, when he could not kill him in this way, put his hands on his throat and strangled him."

This was the story which Evander told to Æneas; and as he told it he showed him the very hill in which the cave had been, and the place where Hercules had pushed down the whole side of the mountain. And now, the feast being finished, two bands of priests, one of old men and one of young, came in and sang a song about the great deeds of Hercules; how, when he was a baby in his cradle, he caught two snakes which Juno had sent to kill him, and strangled them, and how he had killed the Centaurs, who were half horses and half men, and many other wonderful things.

After this Evander took Æneas to his palace—a palace it was called because a king lived in it—and told him all the story of Italy. "Once upon a time," he said, "the people here were savages, not at all better than beasts, not using fire, or living in houses, or wearing clothes, and knowing no difference between right and wrong. Then Saturn came and taught them how to live, and gave them laws."

Then he showed him the city which he had built. A poor place it was; the palace and the temples were of wood or clay, and the roofs were of thatch. But it was the place, though no one knew it, where Rome was to be in the days to come. After this the king took his guest to his home, and showed him the room where he should sleep. So Æneas lay down on a bed of straw, with a bear-skin over him to keep him warm.

THE ARMS OF ÆNEAS

The old man Evander got up from his bed very early the next morning, put on his tunic and his sandals, girded his sword on his side, and, with the skin of a panther over his left shoulder, went to call Æneas. Pallas his son went with him, and two great dogs, which had lain all night by the door of his room, followed him. Æneas he found already awake and dressed, for, indeed, it was not a time when a man who had so much to think about could sleep long.

Evander said: "Great chief of Troy, we have all the good-will in the world for you, but we are poor and weak. There are but few of us, as you see, in this little town, and we can help you but little. Yet there is something which I can do for you; I can tell you of a people with whom you may make friends. They are neither few nor poor; they can help you much, as you also can help them. There is a city not far from this place which was built long ago by men from the land of Lydia; you know the Lydians well, for they are neighbours of Troy and fought for you. Long ago, when there was a great famine in their country, some of them came over the sea to Italy, and built a city, Agylla by name. Now the king of this city, Mezentius, was one of the most wicked of men, and after a while his people made a rebellion against him, and killed his guards, and set fire to his palace. The man himself escaped with his life, and fled to Turnus. So there is war between the people of Agylla—Tuscans they are called—and Turnus; for Turnus wishes to bring back the king and to set him over the people again. But when the Tuscans gathered their army together, and would have gone forth to war, a prophet said to them: 'Tuscans, you do well to be angry with your king, and to fight against him and his friends; but mark this, or you will not prosper,—no man of Italy must be your leader. You must have a stranger to command you.' When the Tuscans heard the prophet say this, they came to me and would have had me to be their leader. But I am old and feeble; and when they would have had Pallas my son, the prophet forbade, because the mother of Pallas was a women of Italy. You, therefore, are the man whom they look for: you are in your prime, and you are altogether a stranger in race. Do you then stand forth and be the leader of these Tuscans. And Pallas shall go with you and learn from you to be a good soldier. Two hundred horsemen I will send with you, and there are two hundred men who follow Pallas my son."

While the king was still speaking there was heard a great clap of thunder, though the sky was clear, and after the thunder the sound of a trumpet such as the Tuscans use. And Æneas knew that these were signs of good; and he said to the king: "Be of good cheer; all shall go well." Then he made ready to go. Some of his company he kept with him; to the rest he said: "Go back to the camp, for they may want you there."

So when he was ready to depart, Evander took him by the hand, and said: "How I wish that Jupiter would give me back the years that are gone. For I, too, was a good soldier in my youth. Did I not kill King Herulus, the man with three lives? Twice I killed him, and he came to life again, and then I killed him for the third time. If I were but such a one now, then either I had gone in my son's place or we had gone together. But now this is my prayer to the Gods: If it be their will that my son should come back safe and sound, then let me live to see him; but if not, then may I die this very day while he still lives and is my own."

When he had said this, he fell back fainting, and his people carried him into his palace.

Then the horsemen rode out from the city, four hundred of them in all, with Prince Pallas in the midst, fair as the Morning Star, the star which is fairer than all others, and which Venus calls by her own name. And they came to a grove where the Tuscans, under their leader, whose name was Tarchon, had pitched their camp.

And Venus had not forgotten her dear son. While he slept, she said to Vulcan her husband: "My husband, while the Greeks were fighting against Troy, I never asked you to make arms for my dear son, as did the goddess of the morning for her son Memnon; and the goddess of the sea for Achilles. For I said to myself: 'The gods have decreed that Troy shall fall: why should he waste his time and his labour in giving help where help cannot be of any use?' But now all things are changed.

My son is come to this land of Italy by the will of the gods; but all the nations are gathering themselves together against him. I pray thee, therefore, to help him and me, that he may the more easily gain that which it is the pleasure of the gods that he should have. Make arms for him that he may conquer his enemies and be safe against their spears and swords."

Very early the next morning, as early as a woman who makes her living by spinning gets up to light her fire and set her servants to work so that her husband and her children may have food to eat, so early did the god of fire rise. He went to a certain island which is near to Sicily, where he had set up his forge. There the one-eyed giants, who were his servants, were hard at work. Some of them were making thunderbolts for Jupiter. Of these thunderbolts one was unfinished, and one could see the things of which it was made. There were three parts of hail, and three of storm-cloud, and three of red fire and of the south wind; and now they were putting in the lightning and noise and fear. Others of the giants were busy with other things. One was making a chariot for Mars, another a shirt of mail for Minerva. But the god cried: "Come, all of you, and do this new work which I have for you. Make arms and armour for the hero Æneas." So they set to work. Some of them melted gold and copper and tin, and some worked at the bellows, and some held the hot metal in pincers, and some dipped it in water.

They made a helmet with a nodding plume that blazed like fire, and a sword, and a shirt of mail, and greaves of gold for the legs, and a spear. But the greatest and most wonderful thing that they made was a shield. For on this the god wrought all the story of Rome and the Romans that were to be. There you might see the she-wolf in the cave of Mars suckling the two babes, for these had been put out to die by a cruel king, and the she-wolf found them, and carried them to her den, and suckled them as if they had been her own young ones. They lay, not fearing her at all, and she was turning her head and licking them as they lay. Also you might see how the Romans were carrying off the Sabine girls to be their wives; in another place there was the battle being fought, where their fathers and brothers came to take them back; in yet another the two kings making peace, so that thereafter the Romans and Sabines should be not two nations but one. Also King Porsenna was to be seen. For the Romans had driven out their king, and Porsenna had come to bring him back. There he stood with his hand stretched out, and on the other side the Romans stood in arms against him. Also the brave Horatius was guarding the bridge by which the enemy would have crossed the river, and the Romans were breaking it down behind him. And yet again the girl Clœlia, having been given as a hostage, had broken her bonds, and was swimming across the river. Also in another place you could see the hill of the Capitol, which, when all the rest of Rome was taken by the Gauls, yet remained. The enemy were creeping up the side, through the trees, and climbing up from rock to rock. Their hair was worked in gold, and so were their cloaks; they carried in each hand a spear, and each had a shield. But at the top the geese were fluttering about, for they were awake, though the very dogs were asleep. They were worked in silver, and the place where they were was worked in gold. And in the middle of the cliff stood the brave Manlius, thrusting down the Gauls just as they laid their hands on the very edge of the cliff. Other things were there to be seen. But the most wonderful of all was the great battle of ships between the East and the West. On one side was Augustus with the men of Italy behind him; on the other Antony, leading to battle Persians and Egyptians and many another barbarous tribe, and close behind him—a shameful sight—his Egyptian wife.

When Venus saw that Æneas was alone, for he had wandered away from his companions, she brought the arms, and laid them at his feet, saying: "These the god of fire has wrought for you. With these you need fear no enemy, no, not Turnus himself." Then she vanished.

NISUS AND EURYALUS

Juno did not fail to see how she might do harm to the Trojans. "Now," said she to herself, "now is the time, while their chief is away, and while their camp is but half-finished." So she sent Iris her messenger to Prince Turnus with these words: "The chance which neither I nor anyone else, whether god or man, could promise you has come of itself, or time has brought it. Æneas has gone away to the city of Evander, hoping to make him his ally. He has left his ships and his camp, which is but half-finished. Take the chance and attack them." Turnus was offering sacrifice, and when he turned about he saw a rainbow, for the rainbow is the way by which Iris goes to and fro, when she carries the messages of the gods. Then Turnus called his army together, and set forth, marching towards the camp which the Trojans had pitched by the sea-shore.

The men who were watching on the wall saw a great cloud of dust, and one of them cried: "To arms, my friends! make ready to defend the camp; the enemy is at hand." Then the Trojans shut the gates, and manned the walls. For Æneas had said: "Do not fight in the plain, whatever may happen: the enemy are too strong for you; keep behind the walls."

Turnus, riding on a Thracian horse, came up to the wall, and threw his spear over it. So he began the siege. Then he rode round the camp, looking for some place where he might make his way in. Just so a wolf will prowl round a sheepfold at night, and the lambs bleat inside, being safe by their dams, and the beast, being wild with hunger, grows more and more mad as he hears them. So Turnus raged round the camp, looking for a weak place by which he might enter. But he could find none, and the Trojans would not come forth. Then he thought to himself: "Well; if I cannot come at them, cowards as they are, I will at the least burn their ships;" for the ships were drawn up by the sea-shore, close to the camp. So he called for torches, and rushed to the ships, holding one ready lighted in his hand, and all the people followed him. Then there happened a very strange thing indeed. Seven years before, when Æneas was building his ships on the plain between the sea and Mount Ida, the mother of the gods said to Jupiter: "My son, you see that Æneas is building himself ships with the pines that grow on my mountain of Ida. This pleases me well; the pines I have given him. But I do not like to think that, being mine, they should be broken by winds and waves when they sail across the seas. Grant, therefore, I pray you, that these ships may be safe against all storms." Jupiter answered: "My mother, you ask what cannot be. Mortal ships cannot be made immortal. They, too, must stand the chances of winds and waves"—and so it was that some were wrecked as Æneas sailed from Sicily to Carthage, and some were burnt in Sicily—"but this you shall have. Such as shall come safe to the land of Italy shall not perish, for I will change them into nymphs of the sea." And so it happened now: before even Turnus and his men could come at the ships, the cables by which they were held were broken, and the ships seemed to move of their own accord, and as they moved they became nymphs of the sea, for every ship a nymph.

All men, Trojans and Latins alike, were astonished to see this thing, and not a little afraid. But Turnus was not afraid: "This," he cried, "is a marvel indeed, but it is a marvel that means ill for these strangers. Their ships flee from us. Yes, and mark you—they will not be able to get away from us. They talk of fate; yes, it was their fate to come to Italy, and it is my fate to destroy them. They are walking in their old ways. Paris stole a wife from Greece, Æneas comes to steal a wife from me. Do they think that this wall will protect them? Did the walls of Troy defend it? And yet these were built by Neptune. And now, who is coming with me to storm their camp? We will not do it in the night; we will not do it by stealth. We do not need a horse of wood to creep into their town. Hector kept back the youth of Greece for ten long years, but the youth of Italy is of another kind."

But by this time it was dark, and nothing could be done. So Turnus set King Messāpus to watch the gate of the camp, and fourteen chiefs of Italy, each with a hundred men, to watch the walls. As for the rest, they sat down to eat and drink.

When it was near to midnight, Nisus, the keeper of the gate—the same that but for his slipping had won the foot-race—said to his comrade Euryălus: "I am bent on doing something this night. Whether the thing comes from the gods, or from my own heart, I do not know, but something I must do. Do you see how bad a watch the enemy are keeping, how some are asleep and some are drunken? Can I not carry the news to Æneas, and so win great honour and reward? Do you see that hill yonder? By that lies the way to the city of Evander."

Euryălus answered: "You are right; it would be a glorious thing to go on such an errand. But you shall not go alone. I will not be left here, O Nisus. My Father did not bring me up to suffer such disgrace, nor have I so behaved that you should think of it. And as for life, who would not die for the chance of winning such honour?"

"Nay," said Nisus, "I did not think for one moment that you would hold back. But this was in my mind. If I come to my end in this affair, then Euryălus will buy back my body from the enemy. Or, if this may not be, he will, at the least, pay the honours that are due to the dead. And then, dear lad, think of your mother. When all the other mothers of Troy chose to stay behind with King Acestes in the land of Sicily, she alone, for she loved you, came with us to the land of Italy."

But Euryălus said: "All this is idle talk. You cannot turn me back, for my purpose to go is fixed. Let us make haste and do the thing." So they roused two of their comrades to take their places, and went to see the chiefs who had the charge of the camp. These were holding counsel together, standing in the open space that was in the middle of the camp, and leaning on their spears. Nisus said: "My lords, I have something to say, and it is a matter that cannot wait." "Speak on," said Ascanius. Then said Nisus: "The enemy are not keeping any watch. Some are sleeping, and others are drunken; the watch-fires are not kept alight. It is in my mind that we two should make our way to Æneas, to the city of Evander. On our way we can kill many of the enemy, and take much spoil from them; but, chief of all, we can tell Æneas of what has happened here. All this we can do easily, if we have but good luck. As for the way, we know it well, for we have hunted in these parts." Then said one of the chiefs: "Troy has not perished altogether, if it still has such sons as you." And Ascanius said: "Bring back my father, and all will be well. As for your rewards, they shall be worthy of you. You, Nisus, if we conquer this land of Italy, shall have the horses and the arms of Turnus, and captives, both men and women, those that you shall choose for yourself, and the land that that now belongs to King Latinus. As for you, Euryălus, you shall come next to myself in all things."

Then said Euryălus: "There is one thing that I would ask. I have a mother. She is of the race of Priam. I cannot say good-bye to her, for I could not bear to see her tears. Do you care for her, if she should lose me." Ascanius said: "She shall be as a mother to me." Then he gave him his own sword with an ivory sheath, and others gave other things to the two. And all the chiefs went with them to the gates, making many prayers and vows for their success. And Ascanius gave them many messages to take to his father.

Then they crossed the ditch which was round the wall of the camp, and went among the enemy. By this time even those who had been set to watch were asleep, for they thought the Trojans to be so weak that there was no need to trouble about them. First Nisus slew a man, Rhamnes by name. He was counted to be a wise prophet who knew what was going to happen, but he did not know of his own death. Then he came to where a chief named Remus lay sleeping; near him were his three servants and the driver of his chariot. All these Nisus killed, and Remus last of all. Many others he slew, and Euryălus coming behind him did the same. But when they came to the tents of King Messāpus, Nisus thought to himself: "We are forgetting our business. The love of killing is too much for us." And he said to his companion: "It is enough: the day breaks; we have made our way through the enemy; let us seek Æneas." So they went on their way. Much spoil they left behind them; but Euryălus put upon his head the helmet of Messāpus, which he had taken from the side of the king where he lay sleeping.

Now it so happened that a certain chief, Volscens by name, was coming with three hundred horsemen from the city to the camp. One of them caught sight of the helmet which Euryălus was wearing, for it glittered in the light of the moon. And he told it to Volscens; and Volscens cried: "Who are you? Whither are you going?"

But the two made no answer, thinking of nothing but how they might escape. So Volscens told his men to watch the wood, which was very thick with trees and brambles. This they did. Nevertheless, Nisus got through it, and might have got away had he wished so to do. But when he came to the stalls where King Latinus kept his cattle, he found that he was alone. Then, for he could not bear to get away leaving his dear companion behind, he entered the wood again and searched it through. After a while he heard the noise of horsemen coming near. So hiding himself in a thicket, he looked, and behold Euryălus was in the middle of the company. He was trying to escape, but could not. Then Nisus said to himself: "May be, if I can kill some of them, the rest, not knowing how their comrades are slain, will be scattered, and Euryălus will escape." So, having first prayed to Diana for help, he threw his spear. The spear struck one Sulmo on the back. It pierced right through him to the very heart, and he fell dead on the ground. While they looked, there came another spear out of the hiding-place of Nisus. This struck another of the horsemen—this time on the head—and killed him. Volscens was furious to see such a thing, that his men were killed he knew not how, and he cried out against Euryălus: "Well, you at least shall suffer for these things," and he flew at him. This Nisus could not bear to see. He came out from his hiding-place, crying: "I am the man who did this: turn your swords on me. He did not, nay, he could not do such deeds. He did but follow his friend." But it was of no use. Volscens drove his sword into the side of Euryălus. In a moment the blood poured out all over him, and his head drooped, like a wild flower in the field when the plough goes over it, or a poppy in the garden when its stalk is broken. When Nisus saw this, he had but one thought in his heart: "Let me die, so that at the least I may kill this Volscens." And he rushed at him, and, for all that his comrades could do to help him, drove his sword right into his mouth and killed him. Then, being himself pierced with many wounds, he fell dead on the body of his friend.

THE BATTLE AT THE CAMP

As soon as it was light the battle began. The Latins had fixed the heads of Nisus and Euryǎlus on poles; these were carried round the camp so that all could see them, and not a little grieved and troubled were the Trojans at the sight. First the Latins tried to take the camp by what was called a "tortoise," because this creature has a very thick and strong shell. Such a shell the soldiers made over their heads, by putting their shields together, and this so closely that no one could thrust a spear through it. Underneath this shield the men worked, some at filling up the ditch and others at digging away the wall. But the Trojans with great labour rolled up a great rock from the inside on to the wall, and this they pushed over so that it fell down upon the "tortoise" and broke it down. Many were crushed to death, and, after this, the Latins were not willing to fight any more in this way. But they did not cease for a moment from attacking the camp. Some put scaling-ladders against the wall, and climbed up by them to the top of the wall. But the Trojans thrust at them with poles and spears as they climbed, killing some and wounding some, and pushing others off the steps of the ladders, so that they fell to the ground. And if one or other did climb to the top and step on the wall, then he was one against many, and could not hold his ground, but was either killed or cast down to the earth. But it was by fire that the great harm was done to the Trojans. There was a great tower upon the walls, which the Latins tried to take, and the Trojans to defend. On to this Turnus threw a lighted torch, and the fire caught the wood of which it was made and climbed from story to story, for the wind was blowing and made the flame the fiercer. In a short time, the lower part being burnt away, the whole tower fell forward, and all the men that were in it perished, except two only. One of them was now growing old, and was but a slow runner, and he, seeing himself surrounded by the enemy, threw himself on to them where the spears were thickest, and so died fighting. But the other was a young man, very nimble and a great runner, and he made his way through the enemy even as far as the wall. And this he climbed, and had now his hand upon the top, when Turnus caught him from behind. As an eagle catches a swan, or a wolf a lamb, so he caught him and pulled him down, and a great bit of the wall with him, for the man clung to the wall with all his might. So the battle grew fiercer and fiercer. Many Trojans were slain and many Latins.

And now came the time when the young Ascanius was to put away childish things and become a man. There was among the Latins a certain Numanus, who was married to the sister of Turnus. This man was not a little proud of himself and of his family, for, indeed, it was no small thing to be brother-in-law to Turnus. So he stood in the front rank and shouted out: "Men of Troy, are you not ashamed to be besieged again? Were not the ten years enough for you? Why were you mad enough to come to Italy? We are a hardy race. We dip our new-born babes in the stream, and our boys exercise themselves with hunting, and our grown men have their hands always either on the sword or on the plough. And when we are old, we do not rest; though our hair has grown white, we still cover it with a helmet. But you, with your mantles of purple, and your long sleeves and your scents, you—Phrygian women, I call you, not Phrygian men—what are you doing here? This is no place for you!"

The young Ascanius could not put up with such boasting. Never before had he used his bow in battle, but only in hunting wild beasts. But now he took an arrow from his quiver, and put the notch upon the string, and drew the bow with all his strength, saying a prayer and making a vow at the same time to Jupiter. Jupiter heard, and thundered on the left hand; and even as the thunder was heard, the arrow hissed through the air, and struck Numanus on the head, piercing it through from temple to temple. "This is the answer, boaster, which the Trojans, twice conquered though they are, send to you." So he cried, and the people shouted for joy. Apollo, where he sat in heaven, looking at the battle, saw the deed. "Go on as you have begun, son of Troy," he cried. But he said to himself: "The lad must not grow over bold." So he came down from heaven, taking the shape of an old man who in time long past had carried the armour of Anchises, and now followed Ascanius. "It is enough," said the old man, "that you have slain this boaster; but now stand out of the battle."

Those who were standing by heard the voice and looked, and as they looked he vanished out of their sight; but they heard the rattle of his quiver, and they knew that it was the Archer-god himself. So they told the boy that he must not draw his bow again. And the battle grew fiercer and fiercer.

Now there were two young men, twin brothers, both tall as pine trees. The name of one was Bitias, and the name of the other was Pandărus. These had been set to keep the gate. And now they opened the gate, and let the enemy come in; but as they came in, the two standing in their places, one on one side of the gate, and the other on the other, struck them down. The Trojans were glad to see it, and grew so bold that they went out beyond the walls, though Æneas had forbidden this, saying: "Whatever may happen, still keep behind the walls." And it would have been well for them if they had obeyed him. For now Turnus himself saw what had been done, and he rushed to the gate. First he killed one of the twin brothers, namely Bitias. It was not by casting a javelin at him that he did it; that had not been enough. He came close to him, and struck him with a great spear that he carried—a great spear with a great point of Spanish iron, a foot and a half long. Through the shield of bull's hide and through a double coat of mail he drove it, and Bitias fell, as a tree might fall, with his shield over him.

When the Trojans saw that their champion was dead, they were troubled, for Bitias was one of the bravest and strongest of them. And Pandărus, in his fear, thrust his broad shoulders against the gate, and shut it again. Some of his own people he left on the outside, but Turnus himself he shut in, not knowing that he had done it. Turnus raged for blood, as a tiger rages when he has leapt into a herd of cattle. And the Trojans fled before him. But Pandărus did not flee. He was not one who was afraid of any man, and, besides, he hoped to have vengeance for his brother. He cried to Turnus: "What are you doing here? This is not your own city; this is the camp of Troy, from which you shall not go out alive." But Turnus laughed to hear him boast, and said: "Begin, if you are so bold; maybe, you have found another Achilles here in Italy." Then Pandărus threw his spear, a great shaft of pinewood with the bark still on it. With great strength he threw it, but aimed it wrong—some said that Juno turned it aside that it struck the gate. Then Turnus raised his sword high above his head, and struck with all his might, rising to the blow. He brought the sword down upon the head of Pandărus, and cleft it in two. Then, indeed, if Turnus had but thought to open the gate and let in his friends, there had been that day an end of the war, and, indeed, of Troy. But he was so greedy to kill that he forgot. Many Trojans he killed, but the gate was still shut, and the Latins could not come in.

But now the Trojan chiefs were ashamed to see that one man could do such harm. They stirred the people with bitter words. "Whither will you flee? What other walls have you? Are you not ashamed to betray your chief? Will you suffer yourselves to be conquered by one man?" Then the Trojans took courage, and joined themselves in a close array, so that Turnus could not choose but give way before them. Just so a lion gives way before a crowd of men. He is frightened, and yet he is fierce. His courage will not suffer him to fly, but when there are so many against him, he dares not stand. So it was with Turnus. Twice he turned, and drove back the Trojans; and twice they pressed him so hard that he could not but give way. His shield was broken, and his helmet bent in, and he himself wearied almost to death. At last, when he came to where the river touched the camp, he leapt into the stream, and swam to the other side.

THE BATTLE ON THE SHORE

While these things were going on at the camp, Æneas made an alliance with the Tuscans under their chief Tarchon. To him he told everything about himself—who he was and whence he came, and how the gods had bidden him settle in Italy. And Tarchon told it to the people, and they, believing that Æneas was indeed the man whom the gods had chosen to be their chief, followed him willingly. So, this matter being settled, he set out on his way back to the camp, for he was not a little anxious about his son and his people. He went first in his ship, and Pallas, the son of Evander, sat by him, and after him came the ships of the Tuscans, and with the Tuscans came others from the northern parts of Italy, some eight thousand men in thirty ships. All that night they rowed down the river, and Æneas sat at the helm of his ship, for his heart was too full of care to suffer him to sleep. About midnight he saw a strange sight. There came up to the side of his ship a nymph. She laid one hand upon the ship, and with the other hand she swam. And he could see that there were other nymphs behind her and by her side. She said: "Are you awake, son of Venus? It is well; there are many things for you to think about. I and my companions whom you see were once your ships, the ships which you built with the pines of Mount Ida. Turnus was going to burn us with fire, and Jupiter changed us into nymphs as you see. Know that your son and your people are besieged in the camp. Put on the armour that the Fire-god made for you, and hasten to help them." When she had said this, she put her hand under the keel of the ship, and pushed it on; and her companions did the same to the other ships. Quickly did they pass through the water, and when the day began to break they were at their journey's end.

Then Æneas passed the word along the fleet, that every one should make himself ready for battle. He himself stood up on the stern of his ship, and lifted his shield in his left hand. Brightly did it flash in the sunshine, and all the Trojans in the camp saw it and were glad, for now, they knew, their chief had come back to them. Turnus also and his men saw it, and were much astonished. For the sea was covered with ships, and Æneas was in the midst of them, and from his helmet and from his shield there shone a terrible light, like the light of a comet when it flares in the sky at midnight. Nevertheless, Turnus did not lose courage for a moment. He said to his men: "Now you have what you wished for. Your enemies do not hide themselves behind walls, but are come to meet you face to face. Think now of your wives and children, and fight for them, to keep them from these robbers. And remember the great deeds which your fathers did in the old time. And now let us make haste, and fight with these men before they can get firm footing on land." So, leaving some of his people to watch the camp, he made all the haste that he could to keep the enemy from landing.

But this he could not do. Some of them had already made their way to the shore, some on planks from the ship's side and some jumping into the sea, where the waves had broken and the water was flowing back, and some running along the oars. As for Tarchon, he spied a place where the sea was calm, and told his men to run the ships upon the beach. This they did. Only Tarchon's own ship was driven on a ridge of rock, and he and all his companions were thrown out into the sea. Still, at last, they all got safe on shore.

Æneas did many valiant deeds. Theron he slew, who was the tallest man in all the army of Turnus. The tallest he was, and he wore a heavier and stronger coat of mail than any other man, but Æneas drove his spear through it. Then he slew the two sons of Melampus, who was the companion of Hercules. They, too, were giants among men; one might have thought that each was a second Hercules, for they fought with clubs, but they could not stand against Æneas. Then seven warriors, sons of one man, came against him. They threw seven spears at him at once. Some of them he caught upon his shield, and some almost grazed his body, but he was not hurt by any. He cried to Achates: "Give me spears enough: that which was good enough for the killing of a Greek, is surely good enough for a man of Italy." And two of the seven he killed. Many others fell dead to the ground both on this side and on that: neither would give way; now a man of Italy was slain, and now a Trojan, for they stood man against man, and which was the bravest no one could say.

In another part of the field Pallas and his Arcadians were fighting. The Arcadians had been used to fight on horseback, but now they were on foot, for they could not bring their horses with them in the ships. When Pallas saw that they fled before the enemy, as men will do when they have to fight in a way which they do not know, he cried: "Now, by the name of your king, Evander, stand firm! Stand, I beseech, if you love me! How shall I show myself worthy of my father, if you are not with me and help me? These are but men whom you see: you fly before them as if they were gods. Follow me, and I will show you where you can win the most renown." So saying, he rushed into the thickest of the fight, and his people followed him. The first that he killed was one Lagus. As the man was lifting a great stone from the ground, he ran him through with his spear. Then while he tugged at the spear to draw it out, another of the Latins thought to slay him. But Pallas turned, so nimble was he and so ready, and struck him full in the breast with his sword, so that he fell dead upon the ground. Then there met him two twin brothers; so like they were that neither father nor mother knew one from the other. But Pallas made a cruel difference, cutting off the head of the one and the right hand of the other.

And now the nymph Juturna—she was sister to Turnus—hastened to her brother, and told him what havoc Pallas was making among the Latins. At once he left the place where he was fighting. As he drove his chariot through the ranks of his army, he cried: "Leave Pallas to me; he is mine: let no one presume to meddle with him." Pallas heard him speak, and looked at him, admiring him, so proudly did he bear himself, and so noble was his look. "This is one worth fighting with," he said. "I shall either win spoils that will make me famous for ever, or shall die with honour." Then he rushed forward to meet the enemy; but his Arcadians stood cold with fear. Then Turnus leapt down from his chariot: he would meet this bold youth on equal terms. Pallas, before he threw his spear, breathed a prayer to Hercules: "O mighty hero, if you remember the house where of old you were a guest, help me to-day. May be I am overbold, to meet so great a chief: yet, if it may be, help me to lay that proud warrior level with the ground and to spoil him of his arms." Hercules heard the prayer, where he sat on his throne in heaven; and it grieved him to the heart that he could not help. Then Jupiter said: "My son, the days of man are but short, and each has his appointed time. But the brave man lives after death by the praise which men give to noble deeds. This youth must die, but he shall not be forgotten. And for Turnus, too, the day of death is near."

Then the two champions met. First Pallas threw his spear. With all his might he threw it. It pierced the shield of Turnus; it pierced his coat of mail; it grazed the skin of his shoulder. And Turnus stood awhile, balancing his spear. Then saying, "This, I think, will do better work," he threw it, and with a better aim. It pierced the shield, the stout bull's hide and the iron, and the coat of mail, and struck Pallas full on the breast. From breast to back it passed, and in a moment he fell dead upon the plain. Then Turnus stood over the dead man, and said: "Men of Arcadia, take this message to your king. I send him back his Pallas. Let him bury his son with all honour—that I do not grudge him; but it has cost him dear that he had Æneas as his guest." So saying, he put his foot upon the body, and dragged from it the belt, a wonderful work heavy with figures wrought in gold. Before many days had passed, he would wish that he had never taken it. Then the Arcadians lifted up the body of their young chief, and laid it on the shield, and carried it out of the battle.

When Æneas knew that Pallas had been slain, and that his people were being beaten in the battle, he made all the haste he could to help them. Many of the enemy he killed, nor would he have any mercy if any of those whom he overcame begged for his life. "No," he cried; "now that Pallas is dead, I will spare no one." So it was when two brothers, who were riding in one chariot, met him. At first they were very bold, and boasted that they would kill him. The one who was driving the horses shouted out: "In the old time, when the Greeks fought against Troy, you escaped. You escaped from Diomed and from Achilles. But you shall not escape from us. The end of your battles and of your life is come." Not a word did Æneas speak, but, before the boaster was ready to fight, he threw his mighty spear. Through the Italian's shield it passed, and pierced his thigh, so that he fell dying from the chariot. "How is this?" cried Æneas, mocking him—"your horses are swift; they do not shy at shadows; they are better than the horses of Diomed or of Achilles: why do you leave them?" Then he caught the horses by the head, and the brother that was left, cried out: "Have pity on me; as you love father and mother, spare me." But Æneas, mocking still, answered:

"Nay, nay, you would not, surely, leave your brother." And he drove his sword into his breast.

When Juno saw that Æneas was driving the Latins before him, and that no one could stand up against him, she said to herself: "This is the man's day of victory; if he meets my Turnus, when he is in this mood, he will surely conquer him." So she made an image of Æneas which seemed to challenge Turnus to battle. And when Turnus made himself ready then the false Æneas fled, and Turnus followed him. To the sea-shore he fled; here there was a ship in which a certain king had come to the war, and the false Æneas seemed to hide himself in it. Turnus, who was close behind, came after, but when he searched he could find no one. While he was looking, Juno cut the cable of the ship, and pushed it out to sea, so that when Turnus looked, the water was round him on every side. Never was man more troubled and ashamed: "O Jupiter!" he said, "what have I done that I should be so disgraced? What will the Latins think of me when they see that I have fled in this manner? How I wish that the waves would swallow me up, or that the winds would drive me to some place where no one would ever see me again!" Three times did he try to throw himself into the sea; three times would he have run himself through with his sword. But Juno would not suffer it, and so brought him safely to the city of his father, King Daunus.

And now King Mezentius came to help the Latins. Wicked as he was, there was no braver man or better fighter in the land. Neither the Trojans nor the Tuscans could stand up against him. He slew Mimas, a Trojan, who was of the same age as Prince Paris, and Actor, who, though he was a Greek, had come to fight for Æneas. From his own land he had come, leaving behind him his promised wife, whose favour he wore in his helmet. Orōdes also he killed, the tallest man in the army of Æneas. Orōdes cried, as he lay dying, "Whoever you are, your end is near; you shall die as I am dying; your grave is ready for you in this land." But the king laughed, for he was one who neither feared god nor regarded man.

But now Æneas saw the king, and made haste to meet him, and the king, on the other hand, did not draw back. "Let others pray to the gods," he said: "my gods are my right hand and my spear." And he threw his spear: it struck the shield of Æneas, but it could not pierce it, so strong was it—was it not made by the Fire-god himself? Yet it was not thrown in vain. Glancing from the shield, it struck one of the Arcadians in the side. The man had been a comrade of Hercules, and now followed King Evander. Then Æneas threw his spear. It broke the shield of Mezentius, and wounded him in the groin, but not to death. And yet without doubt the king would have died that hour, for Æneas drew his sword, and pressed him hard, and he could scarcely move for the spear in his side. But when Lausus, his son, saw in what a strait his father was, he leapt forward, and took the blow of the sword upon his shield. And his companions followed him, with a great shout, and threw their spears at Æneas, and kept him back by force. He would not fly, but neither could he advance. Under the shower of spears he stood, as a traveller stands when a storm falls upon him in the road. Nevertheless his heart was moved when he saw how Lausus came to the help of his father—he also had helped his father in old time. Gladly would he have spared the young man; and he cried to Lausus: "Madman, what do you want? To conquer me? Nay: that is too much for your strength." But Lausus gave him no heed, but still pressed on. Then Æneas grew angry, and the time was come for Lausus when he must die. One blow with his sword did Æneas give him. It cut the shield in two, and broke through the coat of mail, and laid him dead upon the plain. Æneas was sorry to see him lie dead: "What can I do for you, noble boy?" he said. "You had a great pleasure in your arms: keep them: I will not take them; your father, also, shall have your body to bury as he will. It is something, too, that you were killed by Æneas." So he lifted the boy from the ground, and told his comrades to carry him away.

Meanwhile his father sat by a tree on the bank of the river, while his people looked to the wound. He had hung his helmet on a branch, and his arms lay upon the ground. Once and again he asked about Lausus; and he sent a message to him that he should come back. And now his comrades came, carrying the body on a shield. The king saw it while it was yet a long way off, and he knew what it was, and took the dust from the earth, and threw it upon his white hair. "Oh! my son," he cried, "why did I wish so much to live that I let you meet the sword of the enemy in my place? Is it indeed true that you are dead and I am still alive? Ah! my son, now I know that my evil deeds were a shame to you! Oh, that I had died for you, and not you for me! Now I must die, but not yet: there is something that I would first do, if indeed the gods permit—I would avenge my son."

Then he said: "Fetch me my horse." This horse was his pride and joy. From many a battle it had brought him back a conqueror. Very sad was the beast as it came, and the great tears rolled down its cheeks. And the king said: "O Rhœbus, you and I have lived long enough, if anything be for long in this world. To-day you shall bring back the head and arms of Æneas, and we will have vengeance together for our Lausus; or you shall die with me. For a Trojan master you would never, I know, endure."

So he mounted upon his horse, and took a spear in either hand, and rode to meet Æneas. Three times he called out: "I am coming, Æneas!" And Æneas was glad, and cried out: "Are you coming, indeed? The gods be thanked therefor. And now begin." Mezentius answered: "Do not try to frighten me; I can suffer nothing more, now that my son is dead. No: I am come to die; but first here is my gift; take it." And he threw his spear. Spear after spear he threw, but they could not break the mighty shield. And Æneas stood still, watching his time. At the last, he stepped from out the shelter of the shield, and threw his spear. It struck the king's horse full on the head, between the temples. And the horse reared, and lashed the air with his front feet, and fell with his rider beneath him. Loud did the Trojans and the Latins shout when they saw it, those for joy and these for fear. Then Æneas ran, and stood over him, with his sword drawn in his hand: "Where is the great Mezentius now?" he said. And the king answered: "Have done with your threats; slay me; I do not blame you. I never bargained with you for my life, nor did Lausus, my son, when he died for me. Only grant me this. You know that my people hate me. Keep my body from them, and let my son be buried with me in one grave." So he yielded his throat to the sword, and feared not.

THE COUNCIL

The next day Æneas made a great offering to Mars, the god of war. He took a young oak tree, and lopped off all the boughs, and set it on the top of a mound. On this he hung the arms of King Mezentius, the helmet with its crest red with blood, and the spears with their heads broken off, and the coat of mail pierced in twelve places. On the left one branch remained; on this he hung the shield, and on the trunk itself he hung by its belt the sword with its ivory hilt. This done, he called the chiefs about him, and said: "We have done much: this is all that is left of the great Mezentius. But there is more to do. Let us go against the city of King Latinus. This will we do to-morrow. But now let us pay due honour to the dead. We owe very much to them; for have they not bought a country for us with their own blood? And first among the dead is Pallas. His body we will send back to his father."

So he went to the tent where the body had been laid. Old Acœtes, who had been armour-bearer to King Evander, sat watching by the head, and the Trojan women sat on the ground, and wailed and wept. And when Æneas saw the head lying as if in sleep, and the great wound in the breast, he wept. When he could speak, he said: "Surely I hoped that you would see me established in my kingdom, and go back with gifts and honour to your father. But this was not to be. And he may be even now praying for your safe return. Well, at least he will see that you bear your wound in front. But, O Italy! what a son dost thou lose; and you, Ascanius, what a friend!"

So they made a bier of arbutus and oak, and laid the body on it, covered with branches of trees. Like a flower it lay—a violet or a hyacinth which some girl has picked. It has colour and beauty still, but it must fade, for the earth does not nourish it any more. Æneas wrapped one purple robe woven with threads of gold round the body, and another round the head. Some carried the arms which Pallas had won in battle; another carried his helmet and shield—the other arms Turnus had taken; and yet another led his charger. It walked with its head to the ground, and the great tears rolled down its cheeks. Behind these, again, followed the whole company, Trojans and Tuscans, whom Æneas sent to follow the dead. They walked holding their swords and shields with their points to the ground. Æneas said: "The cares and sorrows of war call me: good-bye, my Pallas, good-bye for ever!"

And now there came ambassadors from the city with crowns of olive on their heads, praying for truce, that they might bury the dead. Æneas answered: "You ask for peace for the dead: I would gladly give it to the living. I have come to this land by the will of the gods. Once your King was glad to see me; if now he has changed and would have Turnus for his friend, the fault is not mine. If Turnus is not pleased, let him come forth, and meet me in fight, man to man. When he will, I am ready. But now let there be truce: bury your dead."

So a truce was made for twelve days. And the Trojans and the Latins went up into the woods which were upon the hills, and worked side by side, cutting down trees—cedars and pines and mountain ashes. The Trojans built up great piles of wood upon the sea-shore, and laid on them the bodies of their comrades who had been killed, and on the bodies they put the arms which they had borne in life. The Latins did the same; only they built the piles near to the city. While they were doing this, those who had been chosen to carry the body of Pallas took it to the city of Evander, and there a great mourning was made for him.

When the burning of the dead was finished, there was a great tumult in the city. Many had lost husbands, and many sons, and many brothers. All these cried out against the war: "It is an evil war," they said; "why should we suffer because Turnus wishes to marry the king's daughter? Why does he not fight for her with Æneas, man to man, and so make an end of these troubles?" While they were saying these things the ambassadors who had been sent to King Diomed, to ask for his help, came back. And this was the story which they told, when King Latinus had called the chiefs together, and bade them speak: "We came to Arpi, to the city of King Diomed. The man received us, and asked us why we had come and what we wanted. And when we told him that we wanted him to help us against Æneas and the Trojans, he said: 'Men of Italy, why do you fight against the gods? Do you not know that all of us who fought against Troy have suffered many things? Ajax was struck by a thunderbolt, and Menelaüs was driven to the end of the earth, and Ulysses lost all his comrades and was left alone, and Agamemnon was murdered in his own home! And you see how I am an exile here, for I never saw wife or home again. Fight no more against the men of Troy. You have brought gifts for me; take them back, and give them to Æneas. I have fought with him, and know what he is, with what strength he rises to the stroke of his sword and casts his spear. I tell you this: if there had been in the army of Troy two others as good as he, the Trojans would have come to the very gates of Argos, and Greece would have suffered what she wrought. These two men, Hector and Æneas, bore up against us for ten years, and Æneas is the dearer to the gods, ay, and he is a goddess' son. Make peace with him while you may.' "

So spoke the chief of the ambassadors, and sat down; and there was a murmur in the council, some saying one thing and some another. Then King Latinus stood up and spoke: "This is not a good time for taking counsel; the enemy is outside our walls. Yet hear my sentence. King Diomed will not help us, and you know that twice we have been beaten in battle. We will offer peace. If these Trojans wish to stay in this land, they shall have my kingdom. If they choose to depart, we will build ships for them as many as they want. And now we will send ambassadors with gifts—gold, and ivory, and royal robes, and a throne such as a king might sit on. And Æneas shall choose whether he will go or stay."

Then stood up Drances. He was but feeble in fight, but he was a great speaker and wise in counsel. "You do well, O King, to offer peace. But there is yet something else; all men know what it is, but they dare not say it. Turnus is the man whose pride and self-will are bringing us to ruin. It is he who does not suffer us to speak the truth. But I will speak it though I die for it. Give Æneas these gifts of yours, but add to them another. Give him your daughter, and make peace sure for ever. And you, Turnus, yield this thing. We beg it of you—I, whom you count your enemy, yes, I beg it of you. But if you will not, if your heart is still hard, if you put a royal wife before your country's good, then at the least do this. Do not call on us to die for you and your marriage; meet Æneas face to face."

Then Turnus sprang up from his place in a mighty rage. "You are always full of words, O Drances; when the senators are called together, you are always the first to come and the first to speak. But what have you done in battle? Come, show your courage now. The enemy is close at hand. Let us go and meet him. You hang back, and yet you doubt my courage! Have you not heard of Pallas whom I slew, and of the two brothers who kept the Trojans' gate, and all of whom I laid low when they shut me within their walls? And now, let me say a word to you, my king and father. If you think that it is enough to have been once defeated, if you have no hope that fortune may yet change—be it so: let us pray for peace. Happy the man—that is all that I can say—who shall have died before seeing such foul disgrace. But if we have some strength still left to us; if there are cities and nations who yet will help us; if these Trojans have bought their victory dear, why do we lose courage? Why do we faint before the trumpet sound? Diomed will not help us; but there are princes of Italy as good as he who will fight for us. Even now the great Camilla, with her maiden warriors, is at hand. And for myself—if it please you that I should fight, hand to hand, with this man, let it be so; I do not refuse. Let him be the son of a goddess, and wear the arms which a god has made, I am ready; my life is for my country and my king."

And now, while they were still speaking, there came a messenger with the news that the Trojans were marching from their camp. Great was the uproar. Some cried out for arms, and some cried out for peace. As for Turnus, he shouted: "Call your councils, and talk of peace if you will. The enemy is at the gates, and I go to meet him." And he rushed out of the senate-house.

THE DEEDS AND THE DEATH OF CAMILLA

Turnus gave to all his people the work that they should do. Some should strengthen the walls and the gates of the city, and some should make the trench deeper, and some should follow him into battle. Such as were neither strong nor brave could at least gather a store of stones and stakes. While the men were busy with these things, the women, with the queen and her daughter leading them, went to the Temple of Juno and prayed for help. "Break," said the queen, "the spear of this Phrygian robber, and lay him low before the city."

When Turnus had given his orders, he armed himself, and ran down from the citadel. At the gate there met him Camilla with her maidens, riding on horses, and armed, all of them, for battle. She said to him: "Turnus, stay you here and defend the city. I and my maidens will meet the Trojans and the Tuscans." Turnus answered: "That is well said, lady. I can never thank you enough for the help you give me. But as for the city, it is safe enough. I and my men will lie in ambush in the valley by which this Æneas will approach the city. Do you meet the enemy in front, and I, when the time shall come, will charge them from the side."

Now the story of Camilla is this. She was the daughter of a certain king, Metabus by name, who was driven out of his kingdom by his subjects on account of his cruelty. He fled for his life, taking with him his little daughter, whom he carried in his arms. He came in his flight to a certain river, and the river was swollen with rain, so that it ran high and strong. The man could not swim with the child in his arms, and his enemies were close behind, so he took the spear that he carried on his back, and bound the child to it with strips of bark, and made ready to throw it. As he balanced it in his hand, he prayed to Diana, saying: "O Goddess! I give thee this child to be thy servant for ever, if thou wilt save her now." Then he cast the spear across the river with all his might, and, Diana giving strength to his arm, it fell on the other side. Then he himself leapt into the water, and, swimming across, so escaped from his enemies. After this he never lived in house or town, but with the shepherds on the hills, and the child he fed with mare's milk and the like things. As soon as she could walk he gave her a little javelin to carry, and when she was a little stronger, a bow and arrows. She wore no gold or jewels, nor had she long skirts like a girl. From a child she could sling a stone in a wonderful way, hitting the cranes and the wild swans as they flew high in the air. Tall and strong and beautiful was she when she grew up, and many Tuscan mothers desired to have her for a daughter-in-law, but she had no thought of marriage, only of hunting and fighting.

The goddess Diana, as she sat in heaven, said to Opis, who was chief of the nymphs who waited on her: "Opis, Camilla goes to fight in this war. Would that she had not thought of it! There is not a girl in Italy that I love more, and have loved ever since she was a child. But her fate is on her, and she must die. Now I give you this charge. Go down to the Latin land, where they are beginning just now this evil war; take with you your bow and your arrows, and see that any man who harms her shall himself be slain. And when she is dead no man shall spoil her of her arms; but I will carry back her body to her native land."

And now Æneas and the Trojans came towards the city, the horsemen being in front. One of these, a Tuscan, was the first to kill his man. He charged against a Latin chief, and drove him from his horse, making him fly through the air, as a stone flies from an engine. When the Latins saw him, they turned and fled. And the Trojans and Tuscans followed them. But when they came near the city, then those that stood upon the walls, the old men and the boys and the women, threw sticks and stones at them, and the soldiers took courage and faced about. Then the Trojans, in their turn, fled, and the Latins pursued them. So it happened twice. But when they met for the third time, then neither would the one side nor the other give way. Both of them stood firm, and there was a great slaughter. Many did valiantly, but none was equal to Camilla. Sometimes she would fight with a battle-axe and sometimes with her bow and arrows. Never did she strike a man with her battle-axe but she laid him low upon the earth; never did she aim an arrow at a man, but she killed him. One of these was the hunter Ornytus, who was the tallest of the Tuscans. He had a wolf's head with great white teeth for helmet, and in his hand he carried a hunting spear. But strong as he was, Camilla overcame him, and as he lay dying on the ground she mocked him: "Did you think, O Tuscan, that you were hunting wild beasts to-day? Lo! a woman's arms have brought all your boasts to nothing." So she raged through the field, slaying Trojans and Tuscans alike. One of the Ligurians, the son of Aunus, thought to escape in this way. He said to her: "Let us fight on foot; you have so swift a horse that no one can fight with you on equal terms." Camilla answered: "Be it so; we will fight on foot." And she leapt from her horse, and gave it to one of her companions to hold. But the other turned his horse to flee, foolish man, not knowing that Camilla could run faster than any horse in the world. But so it was; she outran the horse, and stood in front of it, catching the reins in her hand, and so killed him.

Then Tarchon the Tuscan shouted out to his horsemen: "What is this, you cowards? Shall a woman drive you before her? You are ready for the dance and feast, and you lag behind in battle. Follow me." And he rode at Venŭlus, prince of Tibur, and caught him in his arms, dragging him from his horse. So an eagle catches up a snake in his claws and carries him off, and the snake winds himself round the bird, and hisses. Thus did Tarchon carry off his enemy, looking for a place where to strike him, for he was covered with armour, and the man tried to keep the sword from his throat. When the Trojans and the Tuscans saw this, they took courage again.

All this time a certain Arruns, a great archer, was watching Camilla, looking for a chance to kill her. There was a certain priest who was riding in the midst of the battle very splendidly adorned. There were clasps of gold on his armour and the armour of his horse. He wore a purple robe which had come from Tyre; he had a Lycian bow, adorned with gold; his helmet also shone with gold; and his scarf had a ring of gold, and his tunic was rich with the finest needlework. Never was there such a sight to see. And Camilla, having a woman's love of beautiful things, followed him, caring for nothing, and thinking of nothing, but how she might take these splendid spoils. Now Arruns lay in ambush, and when he saw Camilla, how she followed the priest, and thought of nothing else, he said to himself, "Now is the time." And he prayed to Apollo:

"Lord of the bow, help me now, if ever I and my people have done honour to you. I ask no glory for myself. Only let me slay this fury, though I go back to my country without honour." Part of this prayer the god heard and answered, but part was scattered by the winds. For he drew his bow to the full, and let fly the arrow. And when the people heard the twang of the bow, for they could not see the man, they all turned. But Camilla took no heed; she had no thought of the arrow till it struck her under the left breast. She reeled upon her horse, and her companions closed round her and caught her as she fell. Once she laid her hand on the arrow and would have drawn it out, but it had gone too deep. Then her eyes swam in death, and the colour that was as the colour of a rose faded from her cheek. Only as she died, she said, for her thoughts were still with the battle, so keen a fighter was she: "Acca, my sister, tell Turnus to come forth from his ambush, and join in the battle, if he would keep the Trojans from the walls of the city." So she died.

Now Arruns, at the first, lay in hiding, for he was afraid, so great a deed had he done. After a while, he came out from his place, and began to boast. Then Opis drew her bow with all her strength, till the ends came almost together. With her right hand she held the bow-string, and with her left the arrow-head. So she let the shaft fly. Arruns heard the twang, and even while he heard it, he fell dead upon the plain. And now the companions of Camilla flew, as did also the Latins and the allies. The dust of the battle came nearer and nearer to the walls, and a great cry went up to the heaven. Great was the fear and the confusion. Some were trodden down by their own people, so that they died even in sight of their own homes. And the keepers of the gates shut them close, so that their own friends were left outside.

And now Acca had carried to Turnus, as he lay in ambush, the news of how her sister was dead, and how the battle went against his people. Immediately he rose up from his place, and made all haste to the city. And it chanced that at the very same time Æneas had come through the valley and passed over the ridge. The two saw each other; but the night was now falling, so that they could not meet in battle.

THE BROKEN TREATY

That night there was much talk in the city of King Latinus, for the king and Turnus and the queen could not agree among themselves. Nothing would satisfy Turnus but that he should fight with Æneas, man to man. Twice had he seen the Latins and their allies beaten in battle; many of his friends had been slain; and the people looked to him that he should keep his promise, for, indeed, he had sworn that he would meet Æneas in single combat. He said, therefore, to the king, pretending, as men will do, to be more sure of victory than he was in his heart: "My father, these Trojan cowards shall not go back from their word. I will meet this man face to face, and will kill him before your eyes. But if the gods will have it that he should prevail over me, let it be so; you shall be his servants, and Lavinia shall be his wife."

King Latinus was in a sore strait. Turnus he loved, and would willingly have had him for a son-in-law, if the gods had not forbidden. And he would not have him die. Why should he not be content and depart? So he said: "Think awhile, my son; you will have a kingdom in due time, even the kingdom of your father Daunus. And there are other maidens in Italy, noble of birth and fair to look upon, whom you may have to wife. Why will you not be content? I would have given you my daughter Lavinia; but, as you know, the gods forbade. I have been weak, I know; I have changed my purpose, for, indeed, I loved you much, and my wife also moved me with her tears. But see what troubles I and my people have suffered! Twice have we been beaten in battle, and now only the city is left to us, and even this is in danger. If I must yield to these men, why must I also lose you? What shall I profit if you die? Will not my people cry shame upon me, if I suffer it?"

The queen, also, was set against the thought of the single combat. "Oh! my son," she cried, "do not fight with this stranger. What shall I do if you are slain! One thing I know: I will not live to see Æneas my son-in-law."

And Lavinia wept to hear her mother speak in this way, and to think that all this was on account of her. She wept, and her face grew crimson with shame. Her face was as when ivory is stained with crimson, or as when roses are mixed with lilies. Never had she seemed so fair; and when Turnus saw her, his heart burned with love. He turned to the queen, and said: "My mother, do not trouble me with tears and prayers. To this battle I must go." Then he called the herald, and said: "Go to the Trojan king, and bear this message. Turnus says, 'We two will fight man to man to-morrow, and the people shall have peace. And he that prevails shall have Lavinia for his wife.'"

The next day the men of Italy and the men of Troy measured out a piece of ground where these two, Æneas and Turnus, should fight together. In the middle of the ground they built an altar of turf. And the Trojans sat on one side with their allies, and the Latins on the other, with their spears fixed in the earth, and their shields laid by their sides. And all the walls of the city were crowded with women and old men to see the fight.

When everything was now ready, the two kings came to make the agreement. First came Latinus, sitting in a chariot drawn by four horses. On his head he had a crown with twelve spikes which were like to rays of sunlight, for the king was of the race of the Sun. Turnus came in a chariot drawn by two white horses, holding a spear in either hand. And Æneas came, clad in the armour which the Fire-god had made for him, and his son Ascanius by his side.

First, they offered sacrifice on the altar. When this was done, Æneas laid his hand upon the altar, and swore: "If this day the victory shall fall to Turnus, the Trojans shall go to the city of Evander, and shall trouble this land no more. But if the gods shall give the victory to me, then things shall be thus ordered. The Latins shall not serve the Trojans. The two nations shall be equal. King Latinus shall still be king even as he is to-day. The Trojans shall build a new city for me, and Lavinia shall call it after her own name."

King Latinus also laid his hand upon the altar, and swore, calling on the gods that were in heaven and the gods that were below the earth: "Surely this treaty shall stand fast for ever and ever. See this sceptre which I carry in my hand! Once it was the branch of a tree, but a workman closed it in bronze, and made it a sceptre for the king of the Latins.

As surely as it will never again bear twig or leaf, so surely shall this treaty stand fast for ever." But while he was speaking, Juno had it in her mind to break the treaty. She said to Juturna, who was sister to Turnus: "See you how these two are about to fight, man to man? Do you not know how this will end? Do you not see that your brother goes to his death? As for me, I will have nothing to do with this treaty or this fight. But if you can do anything for your brother, now is the time." And when the nymph wept and beat her breast, Juno said: "This is no time for tears: save your brother, if you can, from death. And first cause this treaty to be broken."

Now the Latins, as they sat and looked on what was being done, liked it little. It had seemed to them even before that the fight between these two would not be equal. And now, seeing the two men, that Æneas was bold and confident, and that Turnus walked with his eyes upon the ground, and looked pale and sad, they were more afraid that the fight would go against their own champion. So they began to murmur, and to talk among themselves. When the nymph perceived this, she took upon herself the shape of one Camers, who was a great prince and warrior, and went to and fro among the people, saying: "Are you not ashamed, men of Italy, to allow one man to do battle for you all? Look at these Trojans! See how few they are. There is scarcely one of them for two of you. And if your champion should be overcome how great the shame! He shall gain glory, though he die, but you will suffer disgrace, for whatever the king of these strangers may say, you will surely be servants to them."

And while the man went about among the army, saying these and other like things, there was shown—for so Juno contrived it—a sign in heaven. An eagle drove a great flock of birds before him, and, swooping down from the air to the water, caught a swan in his claws, and began to carry him away. And lo! the flock of birds that had fled from him, turned again and drove the eagle before them, so that he dropped the swan and flew away. Then King Tolumnius, who was skilful in seeing the meaning of such things, cried out: "See you this, my friends? This is such a sign as I have looked for. This eagle is the Trojan stranger; you are the birds: hitherto you have fled before him; now you turn, and he will flee before you."

And as he spoke he threw his spear, and hit one of the men of King Evander below the belt. He was one of nine brothers, sons of a Greek, but their mother was a Tuscan woman. And as his brothers saw him fall dead upon the ground, they caught their spears from where they stood fixed in the ground, and ran forward. So the battle began. First the altar was thrown down, and the wood that was burning on it was taken for firebrands. When King Latinus saw this, he mounted his chariot and fled from the place. Then Messāpus killed the king of Mantua close to the altar, so that he fell dead upon it. And Messāpus cried: "This is indeed a noble offering!" And not a few others were slain, both on this side and on that.

As for Æneas, he stood in his place by the altar, with his head bare, not having either spear or sword in his hand, and cried to the people: "What do you want? Have we not made a treaty? It is not for you to fight. Between you there is peace. The battle is for Turnus and for me."

When he was thus speaking, there came an arrow out of the crowd and struck him in the arm. Who shot the arrow no one ever knew, for no man dared to boast that he had wounded the great Æneas. Then the chiefs led him out of the battle to the camp.

THE DEATH OF TURNUS

Now that Æneas had gone away, Turnus raged more furiously than ever. He drove his chariot right through the host of Trojans, and slew chiefs on either side as he went. One of them was the son of Dolon, who went to spy out what the Greeks were doing in their camp before Troy, and asked—foolish man that he was—for the horses of Achilles as his pay. Turnus struck him to the ground with a javelin, and put his foot upon him and said: "And did you too ask for pay? Take, then, so much of the land of Italy as you lie upon." The Trojans and Tuscans fled before him. Only one man dared to stand up before him—Phegeus was his name. He caught at the bridles of the horses, trying to stop the chariot. But the horses dragged him along, and Turnus thrust his spear through his coat of mail. But Phegeus was not afraid. He loosed the bridles, and, putting his shield before him, made at Turnus with his sword, but Turnus dealt him a great blow where the coat of mail joined on to the helmet, and cut off his head.

Meanwhile Achates and Ascanius led Æneas to the camp. Very slowly did he walk, leaning heavily on his spear. And first he tried to draw out the arrow with his own hand, but could not. Then he sent for Iāpis the physician, and said: "Cut deep; only take out the arrow, and send me back to the battle." Now Iāpis was dear to Apollo; and when the god was ready to give him all his arts, music, and the use of the bow, and to know what was going to happen, he chose rather to have the gift of healing. For his father was an old man and about to die, and Iāpis wished to give him a longer life. And now he did all that he could for Æneas, trying to draw out the arrow from the wound with his pincers, and could not. All the while the battle came nearer and nearer, and the noise grew louder, and the sky was dark with clouds of dust, and the javelins fell thick into the camp. Then Venus, seeing the trouble which had come upon her son, brought him help. It was a healing herb which she knew; the wild goats when they have been wounded by the hunter's arrows seek it out. This she brought, and dipped into the water which Iāpis was using, but no one saw her when she came or when she went. And Iāpis, not knowing what had been done, used the water, in which the herb had been dipped. Immediately the pain ceased, and the blood was stanched, and the arrow came of its own accord out of the wound. Then he said to Æneas: "It is no skill of mine, my son, that has done this. The gods call you to your work." And now Æneas felt that all his strength was restored to him, and he armed himself, and, having kissed Ascanius, went back to the battle. And when his people saw him, they took courage again, and shouted, and charged the Latins and drove them back to the city. Many of their chiefs were slain, among them the man who had broken the treaty; but Æneas would not turn his hand against any. He looked for Turnus, and cared nothing about the others. When the sister of Turnus saw this, she was much afraid; so, running up to her brother's chariot, she pushed the driver from his place, and took the reins herself; but the man did not know what had happened, only he found himself left behind, nor did Turnus know anything about it. She drove the chariot, first to one part of the field, then to another, just as a bird flies about in some room of the house. Æneas saw him, and followed, calling out: "Stop, coward, and fight;" but the nymph turned the horses about and fled away. And once Æneas came near to being killed, for he did not notice how King Messāpus stood ready to throw a spear at him. Just in time he saw it, and dropped on his knee, holding his shield before him. Yet the spear struck the top of his helmet, and cut off the crest. This made him angry, and he ceased to pursue Turnus, and, rushing into the army of Latins, made a great slaughter. After a while it came into his mind to attack the city, for he said to himself: "If I attack the city, surely Turnus will come to help, and we shall meet." So he called to the chiefs, saying: "Come, we will go against the city. I will lay it even with the ground, and its people within it, if they do not keep their promise. As for this Turnus, why should I pursue him?"

Then the whole army made for the walls of the city. Some carried burning torches in their hands, and some scaling-ladders. Some made at the men who kept the gates, and others threw javelins at those who stood on the walls. There was a great strife in the city. Some said: "Let us open the gates, and ask these Trojans to have mercy on us, before it is too late." Others said: "Not so! we will fight for our own city to the last."

The queen stood on the roof of the palace, watching the battle. When she saw how the Trojans were attacking the city, and that her own people were not there to help it, she said to herself: "Turnus is dead, or surely he would be here: it is I who have brought him to his death." And she made a noose out of the purple garment which she wore, and hanged herself from a beam in the roof. When the people knew this, there was great lamentation in the city, and King Latinus rent his clothes and threw dust upon his white hair.

And now the cry of the people in the city was so loud that it came to the ears of Turnus, where he fought in the farthest part of the plain. He caught the reins, saying: "What means this cry from the city? Surely there is trouble. I will go to their help!" But the false driver said: "Nay, my lord, fight here where the gods are giving you the victory. There are enough to defend the city." But Turnus said: "Nay, my sister, for I know who you are, it must not be so. Why did you come down from heaven? Was it to see your brother die? My friends have been slain: shall I see the city destroyed? Shall the Latins see Turnus fly from his enemy? The gods of the living have left me. Receive me, O gods of the dead, for indeed, I have sought to do the thing that is right." While he was speaking, a chief came riding up, his horse covered with foam, and with the wound of an arrow in his face. "O Turnus," he cried, "you are our last hope. Æneas is about to destroy the city, and his men are throwing lighted torches on to the roofs. Only Messāpus and a few chiefs keep up the fight, while you are driving your chariot about these empty fields."

Then Turnus leapt from his chariot, and ran as fast as he could to the city. Where the blood ran deepest on the earth and the arrows were flying thickest in the air, he ran. He beckoned to his men, and cried: "Stay your arrows; stand still; I am come to fight for you all." When Æneas saw it, he left attacking the city, and came to meet his enemy. Both the armies stood and looked, for, indeed, they were two mighty chiefs.

First they cast their spears at each other; then they ran together, and their shields struck together with a great crash. First Turnus rose to his height, and struck a great blow with his sword, and all the Trojans and all the Latins cried out when they saw him strike—these with hope and those with fear. But the treacherous sword was broken in the blow. And when Turnus saw the empty hilt in his hand, he turned to fly. They say that when he mounted his chariot that day to go to the battle he left his father's sword behind him, not thinking what he was doing, and took in its place the sword of his charioteer. This served him well enough while he was fighting with others, but when he came to the shield which the Fire-god had made, it broke like ice. So Turnus fled, and Æneas, though he was yet somewhat hindered by his wound, pursued him. And Turnus cried out: "Give me a sword." But Æneas cried: "If any one helps him I will burn the city to the ground." Five times round the space between the two armies they ran, and Turnus could not escape, nor could Æneas take hold of his enemy. Now there stood in the plain the stump of a wild olive tree, and it was sacred to the god Faunus. In this the spear of Æneas had fixed itself when he cast it at Turnus but had not hit him. Now he tried to pull it forth. But Turnus cried to the god: "O Faunus, if I have kept sacred the things which the Trojans have profaned, hold fast this spear." And so it was, for Æneas could not draw it forth. And while he struggled with it, the nymph, the sister of Turnus, taking the form of the charioteer, ran up, and put his own sword into his hand. When Venus saw this, she, too, came down, and drew the spear from the stump.

Then said Jupiter to Juno, as they sat watching the battle: "How long wilt thou fight against fate—What wilt thou? Was it well that the nymph should give back to Turnus his sword? Thou hast driven the Trojans over land and sea, and filled Italy with death, and turned the marriage song into mourning. Further thou must not go."

And Juno answered humbly: "This is thy will, father of gods and men, and I yield. But grant me this: do not let the Latins be called by the name of Troy, or change their dress, or their speech. Let Rome rule the world, but let Troy perish forever."

And Jupiter answered: "It shall be so; all that thou askest I will give. The Italians shall not change name, or dress, or speech. The men of Troy shall become Latins, and by none wilt thou be more honoured than by them."

And now Æneas came on shaking his great spear. "Why do you draw back, O Turnus?" he said. "If you can, fly through the air, or hide yourself in the earth; but if not, meet me face to face." Turnus answered: "It is not you I fear; it is the gods who are turned against me." Then he turned to fight. His sword he did not use, but he saw a great stone that lay close by, the landmark of a field. Very great it was, so that twelve men—such as men are nowadays—could scarcely lift it from the ground. This he caught from the earth, and, running forward, cast it at Æneas. But he scarcely knew what he was doing, for his knees tottered beneath him, and his blood was cold with fear. He was like to a man in a dream, who tries to run and cannot. The stone fell short, and then Turnus looked about him. He saw the city, but his chariot he could not see, nor his sister. He could not fight, and he could not flee, and the dreadful spear was pointed at him. For a while Æneas stood shaking it in his hand, waiting till his aim should be sure. Then he threw it with all his might. It came like a whirlwind, and pierced the seven folds of his shield, and made a deep wound in his thigh. And Turnus dropped with his knee on the ground, and all the Latins groaned aloud to see it. Then he said: "I have deserved my fate: take what you have won. And yet have mercy on me. Pity the old man, my father. You had such a one for your own father. Give me back to my own people. They have seen me beaten; they see me beg my life from you: Lavinia is yours. Therefore spare my life."

And Æneas stood in doubt. He might have spared him, but that his eye fell on the belt of Pallas. Then he cried with a dreadful voice: "Shall I spare you when you wear the spoils of my friend? Not so; take this; it is Pallas slays you." And he drove his spear into his breast. So the spirit of Turnus passed into the darkness.

AFTERWARDS

So Æneas married the fair Lavinia, and built a city which he called after her name. This city soon grew to be a great place, for the people in the country round about heard the fame of the great Æneas, how brave he was in battle, and how just, and they came in great numbers to be his subjects. Yet he had enemies, for those whom he had overcome in war wished to be revenged, nor did they like that a man from foreign parts should rule over them. So they gathered a great army together, and marched against the new city. Æneas went out to meet them, and put them to flight; but he never came back to his city. Some said that he was drowned in a river which runs into the sea not far from those parts; others, that his mother Venus carried him away. Certainly he was never seen again by any man.

By this time Lavinia had a little son, and Ascanius thought that it would be well to leave the city Lavinium to his young brother, and to found a new one for himself. There were, indeed, by this time so many people, Trojans, and Latins, and Tuscans, and Greeks, who had come from the city of Evander, that one place was not big enough to hold them. So Lavina had charge of the city which had been called after her, till her son should be old enough to take the kingdom, and Ascanius built a new town for himself, and called it Alba Longa—that is, the Long White Town.

Not long after this the old King Evander died, and as he left no son to succeed him, the little town which he had built among the seven hills by the Tiber was deserted, and the people joined themselves either to Ascanius at Alba, or to Lavinia and her son at the other city.

For many years the place was without inhabitants. Then by degrees a little village grew up. For one thing, the country about Alba was not a little troubled with earthquakes, but these did not reach as far as the valley of the Tiber. People, too, who got into trouble at home, were often glad to flee to this out-of-the way place across the river.

Then a wonderful thing happened: just what the Fire-god had shown on the shield which he made for Æneas. Two babies, children of a princess descended from Æneas, were left out to die by a cruel uncle; but a she-wolf which had lost her own cubs suckled them, and they grew up to be the strongest men in the country. As time went on the village was turned into a town, and the town was made a strong place. The people who lived in it called themselves Romans. Some of their neighbours they conquered, and with some they made friends. Little by little they made wider their boundaries and increased their power. Many troubles they had, from quarrels among themselves and from enemies without. More than once their city was taken. Still, however low it fell, it rose again stronger than before. It conquered first all Italy, and then the countries nearest to it, and then far-away nations in Asia and Africa. Our own island of Britain was almost the last of its conquests. We may still see the ruins of the splendid houses which the Romans built here, and the camps which their soldiers made. Most wonderful of all the things which they left behind them is the great Wall which was made right across the island to keep out the savages of the North. "Most wonderful," I say, but still greater than this was what we have from them of Law and Order. But this is a matter of which you will hear more when you are older.

Made in the USA
San Bernardino, CA
06 August 2019